TALES FROM THE
KENTUCKY
HEMP HIGHWAY

TALES FROM THE
KENTUCKY
HEMP HIGHWAY

DAN ISENSTEIN

THE
History
PRESS

Published by The History Press
Charleston, SC
www.historypress.com

Front cover, bottom: National Archives, ID 20191122. Series: War Hemp Industries, 1942–1946.
Back cover, top: courtesy of the National Archives, ID 204375634. Series: War Hemp Industries, 1942–1946.

Unless otherwise indicated, all images are courtesy of the author.

First published 2021

Manufactured in the United States

ISBN 9781467148832

Library of Congress Control Number: 2021938371

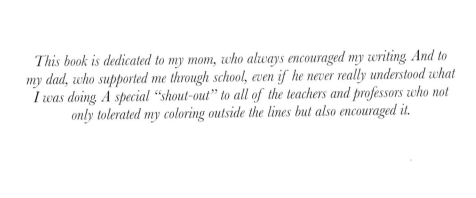

This book is dedicated to my mom, who always encouraged my writing. And to my dad, who supported me through school, even if he never really understood what I was doing. A special "shout-out" to all of the teachers and professors who not only tolerated my coloring outside the lines but also encouraged it.

CONTENTS

FOREWORD

The history of America is the history of hemp; they are inextricably entwined. Since Jamestown in 1610, even before America was America, the government mandated its cultivation and allowed taxes to be paid in hemp stalk. The seed of choice for western expansion, still today, thousands of acres of hemp are near streams and rivers throughout the Midwest. The source of canvas for wagons and ropes for mines, rigging for ships and fodder for animals—without hemp, could there even be an America as we know it today? The War of 1812 was fought over it, and Mormon founder Joseph Smith demanded that it be planted: "grow hemp or go naked." Fancied as a component in Henry Ford's cars, his company even grew it in Michigan. Despite the USDA's "Hemp for Victory" campaign, the crop was caught up in laws designed to continue the enslavement of people of color via prison sentences. Hemp was not truly free from 1937 until the Farm Bill eighty-one years later. And for most of American history, Kentucky was ground zero for the cultivation and development of hemp and its "25,000 products." Read here that proud and robust history.

—Richard Rose,
"The Richard Rose Report"

PREFACE

I refer to my work as "history lite." The purpose is to make a topic engaging to the casual reader while at the same time whetting the appetite of more inquisitive readers for their own dig into any individual narrative. Kentucky hemp history is so entwined with the overall state narrative that a work of this nature cannot possibly be undertaken without glaring omissions. This is especially so in the chapter about Lexington/Fayette County, the capital of Kentucky's "hempire." Names like Thomas and Nathaniel Hart and Thomas and Peter January are conspicuous in their absence.

In other places, seemingly minor stories are used to indulge in deeper explorations of topics such as the binder twine boom of the 1890s or the "Billion Dollar Crop" era of the 1930s. Likewise, the relationship between hemp and slavery is explored in several places.

No one book could possibly explore all aspects of the hemp industry's impact on the development of the Commonwealth of Kentucky. This volume is an initial attempt to share over two hundred years of "hempstory." There is so much more to discover.

ACKNOWLEDGEMENTS

Too many people assisted in this project or provided some sort of support to thank them all. Jenny Leslie and Trent Rogers provided valuable feedback to the manuscript and listened to me ramble; Mike Robinson, Marla Rivera, Bill Reinke and Stephen Ackerman. Eric James and Michael Denis helped researching Danville/Boyle County. Ted Spears was incredibly patient, and his donation of the family business records to the University of Kentucky provided access to information that in some cases has not been viewed in over one hundred years. They help make this book unique. I am truly grateful to have facilitated this donation. Richard Rose, who wrote the foreword and has been a source of support and guidance since I embarked on my journey into hemp. Harry Enoch helped compile the hempstory of early Clark County. Thanks also to: Sandy Stultz and the staff of the

Hempfield at University of Kentucky Research Farm during the Pilot Program Field Day 2015.

Bluegrass Heritage Museum in Winchester; Tandy Nash at the Gateway Museum in Maysville; Julia Taylor at the Scott County Public Library; the Woodford County Historical Society; Melody Williams of the Danville Public Library in Danville, Illinois; Julie Kemper at the Kentucky Historical Society; Foster Ockerman, Beth Crosby, Kent Brown, who befriended me early in my attempt to make Kentucky's hemp history a bigger story and with whom I am coproducing a documentary on U.S. hemp history; the Jessamine County Historical Society; Megan Mummy and the staff at the University of Kentucky's Special Collections Library; the staff at the Capital City Museum in Frankfort, who made the connection between Paul Sawyier and Kentucky River Mills; John Dvorak; Chad Rhoad and Rick Delaney, my editors at The History Press; and countless others who have supported and encouraged this project.

INTRODUCTION

Why a book about Kentucky's hemp industry structured around roadside historical markers that mention hemp? Celebrated Kentucky historian Thomas D. Clark provides the answer: "The production of hemp historically bore a close relationship to the economic, social and political history of the Commonwealth."[1] In other words, Kentucky's "hempstory" is a narrative thread woven throughout all aspects of Kentucky life and state history.

There are currently fourteen historical markers (at least three are missing) in twelve Kentucky counties touching on the state's hemp industry. Ten of these markers share a side with similar content. The following passage is a synthesis of that shared content:

> *Hemp in Kentucky—First crop grown, 1775. From 1840 to 1860, KY's production largest in U.S. Peak in 1850 was 40,000 tons, with value of 5,000,000. Scores of factories made twine, rope, oakum to caulk sailing ships, gunny sacks, bags for cotton picking and marketing. State's largest cash crop until 1915. Market lost to imported jute, freed of tariff. As a war measure, hemp grown again during World War II.*[2]

In seven brief sentences, these ten signs that share a common side communicate 170 years of Kentucky history. In doing so, the markers reference the frontier, antebellum Kentucky, the turn of the twentieth century and the Second World War.

"Hemp in Kentucky," a common sign at the back of many roadside historical markers, which share over 175 years of Kentucky hempstory.

Kentucky's hempstory is like a weed growing in the cracks of the broader historical narrative. It sprouts up among the names and stories populating Kentucky history. Daniel Boone Bryan, Daniel Boone's nephew, established a successful hemp plantation in southern Fayette County. John Wesley Hunt, the first millionaire west of the Allegheny Mountains, was a pioneering hemp industrialist. Senator Henry Clay crafted federal policy to the benefit of the domestic hemp industry, including his own interests.

The success of Kentucky's hemp industry depended on the labor of enslaved people. This dependence influenced Kentucky politics until the Civil War. Abraham Lincoln's opposition to slavery was galvanized during a visit he made to Farmington, a hemp plantation in Louisville, in 1841. John Hunt Morgan, John Wesley Hunt's grandson, went to war to defend his right to enslave the people who worked in his hemp factory.

Even after the Civil War, hemp remained Kentucky's largest cash crop. Between 1880 and 1915, Kentucky hemp helped feed the demand for agricultural binder twine. After the First World War, hemp began a long, slow fade from the state's agricultural and industrial landscape. But, like a spectacular sunset, Kentucky hemp enjoyed one last glorious moment during World War II. The sun finally set on Kentucky's historic hemp industry in 1952, when Kentucky River Mills closed.

A hempen thread binds over 175 years of Kentucky history. The question really ought to be, "Why wasn't this book written earlier?"

1
WHAT IS HEMP?

H emp is quite possibly the oldest cultivated crop in human history. As Chris Conrad observed in *Hemp: Lifeline to the Future*: "Hemp was the first plant known to be cultivated. About 10,000 years ago, hemp industries appeared simultaneously in China and Eurasia for the production of hemp fiber."[3] Archaeological evidence from the Oki Islands in Japan suggests that hemp seed was part of an early human diet.

But that still does not explain what hemp is. That question may best be answered by agronomist Lyster Dewey, whose essay about hemp culture appeared in the *Yearbook of the United States Department of Agriculture: 1913*: "Hemp belongs primarily to the plant *Cannabis Sativa*. It has long been used to designate the long fiber obtained from the hemp plant."[4] Dewey notes that the word *cannabis* appears as a unique word in eighteen languages, reflecting hemp's significance across cultures.[5] At the time, Dewey noted that the word *hemp* was often used interchangeably to describe fibers from a variety of plant sources, including, abaca, sisal, henequen and jute, among others. However, the term did not extend to flax, "which is more like hemp than any other commercial fiber."[6] According to Dewey, hemp "belongs to the mulberry family, Moraccae…and the hop." And it is also "closely related to the nettle family."[7]

In the ten thousand years that hemp has been utilized by humans, it has spread around the globe. In 1913, Dewey documented fourteen countries across four continents that cultivated hemp fiber in significant amounts. Of those fourteen countries, four produced enough hemp to support exports.[8]

Hemp is a "bast fiber." Bast fibers are harvested from the phloem, or vascular tissue, of a plant. Other bast fiber plants include flax, nettle, jute, kenaf and kudzu. Hemp fiber is one of the longest, strongest and softest of the bast fibers.[9] It is also extremely versatile. At various times, it has been used to make thread, yarn, rope and cordage. Some of these products are further processed into textiles of various quality, from fine linen and sail cloth to "duck" canvas and agricultural bagging.

Hemp is particularly well suited for marine applications and was the preferred raw material for sail cloth, ship rigging and anchor lines. Centuries before the first steamship, hemp harnessed the wind and powered the age of exploration and colonization.

This incredible versatility made hemp a desirable crop on the frontier. Hemp culture was pivotal in Kentucky's evolution from unexplored wilderness to pioneer homesteads and, eventually, the Commonwealth of Kentucky. "The hemp industry began in Kentucky with the establishment of the first permanent homes in the wilderness."[10] When the frontier opened, "families were impelled by circumstances to manufacture cloth from fibers native to their new homeland."[11] In a story recounted by Daniel Boone's son Nathan, the family would "gather nettles, a sort of hemp, towards Spring, when it became rotted by wet weather."[12] The nettle fiber, or lint, could then be spun into thread. Hemp, flax and cotton were viewed as essential crops once land was cleared.

Hopkins speculated that "pioneer housewives often thought lovingly of the hemp, cotton and flax of the seaboard and planned to have them produced on their own...as soon as possible."[13] For pioneers, hemp production supplied the raw material to meet "domestic needs for clothing, linen and rope."[14] Hemp was also considered a commodity and a cash crop for Kentucky farmers who often used the fiber in trade with local pioneer merchants.

Basic hemp production focuses on the separation of hemp fiber from the hemp stalk. Raising hemp for fiber was extremely laborious and time consuming. The crop, usually planted in mid- to late May, grows quickly, choking out weeds. Historically in Kentucky, hemp was harvested by hand using a "primitive reaping knife, called a hemp hook."[15] Experienced field hands used some variation of this method: "In cutting the left arm should be thrown around the hemp, so as to gather it near the top, under the arm and next to the body; the knife, held in the right hand should then be applied in the opening which is thus made in the hemp, and so much as gathered should be cut close to the ground, with a steady drawing motion, and not

Hand looms were used on the frontier to weave textiles of hemp, cotton, flax and wool.

with a violent stroke."[16] Manually, an experienced field hand could harvest half an acre per day.

After it was cut, the hemp needed to "ret," or rot. The enzymes produced during the retting process break down the gummy substance that binds the fiber in the stalk.[17] There were several ways to ret hemp. Kentucky farmers primarily used a process called "dew retting," in which the cut hemp was laid in rows in the field and allowed to dew rot for several weeks. Periodically, laborers turned the hemp to promote even rotting. After the hemp was sufficiently retted, it was stacked into shocks to be broken in the field by laborers.[18]

Dew retting produced an inconsistent fiber, as the process was somewhat dependent on the weather. The fiber also often had a dingy or dirty appearance from being left on the ground. In Kentucky's peak hemp production years, most of the crop was consumed by local manufacturers for the production of agricultural bagging and baling materials.

Another popular method for rotting hemp was to immerse the cut hemp in pools of water. This method is called "water retting."[19] Water retting produced a superior product, especially for making rope and sail cloth. This was the common practice in Russia, which exported hemp fiber known as "Riga reign." Considered the industry gold standard, Riga reign was the preferred grade of hemp for rigging and outfitting naval vessels, including those of the United States, Britain and France.

After the hemp was properly prepared, "the farmer devoted his attention to separating the lint from the wood, a task accomplished by 'breaking' the

Hand hemp brake, or break, used for separating hemp fiber from the stalk. Used in Kentucky into the early twentieth century.

stalks and 'hackling' the fiber." In Kentucky, enslaved people used a device called a "hemp brake" to process hemp stalks.[20]

> *The laborious task of hemp breaking began as soon after Christmas as possible in order that it might be completed before the arrival of the season for spring plowing. The brakes were moved from shock to shock over the field to avoid the necessity of carrying the hemp straw, and often the operator kept a fire burning nearby for the double purpose of keeping himself warm and of drying the hemp.[21]*

It was dirty, backbreaking work that also required significantly more skill than was often acknowledged.

> *Holding a small bundle of stalks in his left hand, he placed their tops across the lower slats of the brake, then with repeated strokes brought the upper arm down sharply upon them. This shearing action broke the wood into small pieces, called hurds or shives, which were shaken out by whipping the bundle against the machine or against a stake or striking it with a paddle. By continuing the process of alternately breaking and whipping the lint was freed from the wood along its entire length.[22]*

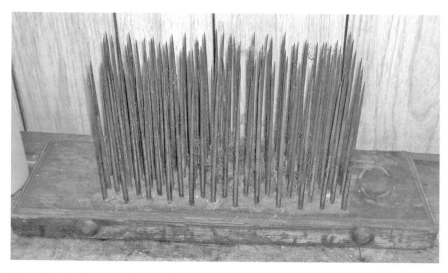

Hemp "hackles" were used to comb hemp and flax fiber.

Hemp was a vital raw material to the Kentucky economy, as it was processed into value-added products. Some of the earliest industries on the frontier converted staple crops like corn into whiskey and hemp into rope, oakum and, later, agricultural baling materials.

Kentucky manufacturers seized the opportunity created by the cotton boom in the Deep South. Rapid industrialization in central Kentucky was fueled by the production of baling materials in the form of hempen bagging and baling cord, to support the cotton industry.

2

BOYLE COUNTY

First Crop

The marker commemorating Kentucky's first hemp crop is located in Boyle County. The narrative on this marker introduces the importance of hemp on the frontier. The marker celebrates original pioneer Archibald McNeill, who planted Kentucky's first recorded hemp crop in 1775.[23]

> *Kentucky's first recorded hemp crop, 1775, was on Clark's Run Creek, near Danville. Grown by Archibald McNeill, who brought the first seed with him when he located here. Hemp production spread slowly throughout the area, but Boyle County later became one of ten Bluegrass counties which together produced over 90 percent of entire US yield in 1889.[24]*
> *—Marker 1279, Boyle County Courthouse, Danville*

McNeill's introduction of Hemp culture in Kentucky can be directly traced back to the establishment of the first permanent settlement in the territory. So, how does McNeill come to Kentucky, and what happens to him after he plants that first hemp crop in 1775?

In 1754, at the start of the French and Indian War, Kentucky was part of North America claimed by France. The French surrendered these claims to the British in the Treaty of Paris, which ended the war in 1763.[25] While the British agreed to limit settlement in the lands ceded by France, the acquisition of new territory initiated a rush by colonials to scout, survey and claim it. Virginia veterans in particular believed their service should be compensated in the form of "western bounty grants"—land—in the newly acquired territory.[26]

Window moldings on the 300 block of Main Street hint at Danville's hemp history. Such architectural details are often salvaged from other buildings.

Despite the interest, permanent settlement in Kentucky was not attempted by Whites until 1774. That summer, James Harrod and thirty-one men traveled by canoe down the Ohio River. They entered the mouth of the Kentucky River and paddled upstream to what is now Mercer County, where they disembarked and hiked inland. By June 16, 1774, they had erected the first "permanent" cabins in the territory. This activity attracted the attention of local Indian tribes; a raiding party ambushed a group of five settlers who were clearing trees on July 20, 1774. One of the men, Jared Cowan, was killed, while Jacob Sandusky and another man fled down the Cumberland River, eventually making it to New Orleans. The fifth settler returned to the fort to report the attack.[27]

Concurrent to these events, famed frontiersman Daniel Boone arrived at the settlement with a message from Lord Dunsmore, the colonial governor of Virginia. Because of recent Indian activity in the territory, Dunmore put out a call for men to form a militia regiment.[28] The ensuing military campaign, appropriately named "Dunmore's War," was decided on October 10, 1774, at the Battle of Point Pleasant. The Indian defeat resulted in the loss of their hunting rights in the Kentucky territory.

That winter, Harrod made plans to return to Kentucky. In February 1775, Harrod's scouts reconnoitered the area and found no evidence of Indian activity. On March 11, Harrod, this time with fifty-four men, returned to Kentucky and began reclaiming the cabins.

Included in Harrod's second group of men was Archibald McNeill.[29] There is no record indicating if McNeill was part of Harrod's original group of thirty-one men that attempted settlement in 1774. Regardless of when he joined Harrod, McNeill brought a valuable commodity with him: hemp seed. Not long after returning to the settlement, Archibald McNeill planted the first recorded hemp crop in the Kentucky territory.

Lewis Collins makes an interesting distinction in his *History of Kentucky*. In the chapter "First Things in Kentucky," Collins writes, "The first *seed hemp* was raised in 1775, by Archibald McNeill, on Clark's Creek not far from Danville."[30] The wording appears deliberate, potentially implying more than just Kentucky's first hemp crop. Hemp seed would have been an extremely valuable commodity on the frontier. Was McNeill growing a crop of seed hemp for sale or use in the following season?

Sadly, Archibald McNeill did not survive the frontier for very long. In 1779, a clerk with the Fincastle County, Virginia court traveled to Kentucky to register land claims. Among the registered claims recorded at Fort Harrod on November 3, the clerk's office issued Peggy McNeill confirmation of her settler's claim. It was made in the name of her husband, Archibald McNeill, who is listed on the claim as "deceased."[31]

Collins published his original volume in 1847, a peak period for Kentucky's hemp industry. When Collins compiled his research, the significance of the state's hemp industry was undeniable. The impact of the industry is reflected

"First Crop" Roadside historical marker, Boyle County Courthouse, Danville, Kentucky.

Grayson's Tavern, the site of early Kentucky political activity, is part of a collection of frontier-era buildings. Constitution Square, Danville, Kentucky.

throughout the entire volume. In each county summary, he included up-to-date demographic and economic information. This information included the population of freed men and enslaved people, staple crops (including hemp) with annual output, as well as the number and types of merchants and businesses. Significantly, Collins made sure to mention ropewalks and bagging factories as signs of economic development. His clear understanding of hemp's significance to the state narrative suggests that his use of the term *seed hemp* was deliberate.

McNeill may be credited with planting the first recorded hemp crop in Kentucky, but his is not Boyle County's only compelling hempstory.

> *Boyle County was formed from parts of Mercer and Lincoln in 1841 and named for the Honorable John Boyle, for many years the chief justice of the state....The soil of this county is very deep and rich, and generally lies well for cultivation. The products are principally stock and hemp. The citizens are generally independent in their circumstances well educated and intelligent.*
>
> *The towns of Boyle County are Danville and Perryville....Danville was established by the Virginia legislature in 1787, and was for many years the seat of government of Kentucky.[32]*

25

THE CROW BARBEE HOUSE

John Crow was one of Harrod's original thirty-one men on the abandoned 1774 expedition. On their arrival at the spot they intended to settle, Harrod drew up lots, which the men selected to determine who would homestead on each one. Crow and James Brown drew neighboring lots along Clark's Run Creek. Crow later sold his lot to James Wright in 1781. Unfortunately, Wright was killed by Indians before he and his family moved in. In turn, Wright's heirs sold the property to Thomas and Joshua Barbee in 1784.

Thomas Barbee was born in Virginia about 1752, the oldest of five siblings. When Thomas was seventeen, he impregnated one of the family's enslaved women. This resulted in the birth of his daughter, Lydia, in 1768. Thomas's stepmother was furious and threatened to tell his father. Fearful of his father's reaction, Thomas ran away and lived with a cousin for a time. He later enlisted in the Continental army during the Revolutionary War, serving alongside his father and other family members.[33] Part of the compensation for enlisting in the regular army came in the form of "land grants" in the western territories. Because Barbee rose to the rank of captain, he was entitled to claim one thousand acres in the western Virginia territory of Kentucky.

Following the war, Thomas Barbee, his brother Joshua and their families migrated to Kentucky. They bought Wright's property in 1784, renaming the estate Oakland.[34] The Barbees grew hemp and engaged in various business pursuits. Their relative success was indicated by the improvements they made to the small stone house on the property. Thomas also started indulging other interests. In 1789, he and his brother were investors in "The Kentucky Society for the encouragement of Manufacturers," also known as the "cotton factory." The ill-fated venture to manufacture cotton cloth and stockings apparently went bankrupt having never manufactured any products.[35] Along with the Crow property, Barbee also built a house "in town," near Grayson's Tavern.

When Thomas Barbee settled in Kentucky, he brought along his daughter Lydia, who was still his property. Thomas married twice but failed to have children with either wife. Lydia was his only child. Lydia married a Tuscarora Indian named Dennis Doram. The couple had several children, including Dennis Doram Jr., who was born in 1796.[36]

Thomas Barbee died on February 22, 1797. In his will, he decreed that Lydia, his grandchildren and their progeny would all be "free persons" when they reached age. The will stipulated that the women were to be

Crow-Barbee House, Danville, Kentucky. It was purchased by Joshua and Thomas Barbee in 1784 and named "Oakland."

emancipated when they reached the age of twenty-six, the men at age thirty-one. Additionally, Barbee's will and testament stipulated that all of his descendants were to be educated.[37] This was in 1797, when women were not generally educated. Kentucky was one of the few slave states where educating Black people was not criminal.[38] Lydia and her children were Barbee's only progeny. His actions indicate some affinity for them.

His grandson Dennis Doram Jr. put his education to work and quickly established himself in business. He married Diadaemia Gibson of St. Louis in 1830.[39] Diadaemia was born in Washington County, Kentucky, to Chloe Taylor, an enslaved woman, and Gibson Taylor, a free man. Chloe and the children were sold to a family in St. Louis. Gibson Taylor was eventually able to buy his family's freedom for $700.[40]

Dennis and his brother Daniel partnered on various businesses, including a ropewalk they operated between 1835 and 1839 in Danville.[41] Dennis also acquired approximately 450 acres of land on the Dix River and several downtown lots. He is reported to have operated as many as three ropewalks, one in Danville, one in Shelby City and another in Goresbury.

His intelligence and attention to detail helped him to become the "wealthiest man of his race" and a leading citizen of Danville.

Records also indicate that the Dorams owned several enslaved people over the years. Some evidence suggests that Dennis may have entered into contracts with his enslaved people that allowed them to earn their freedom.[42]

JONATHON NICHOLS

In 1804, Rhode Island rope maker Jonathon Nichols received a job offer to be the superintendent of a ropewalk in Danville, Kentucky. Jonathon saw an opportunity to build something on the frontier and set off for Kentucky. He wrote to his family of his journey and life in Danville in a series of letters.

Just twenty-one years old when he left Newport, Nichols was described as "an extremely industrious, ingenious, modest, amiable young man."[43] He started his journey from Newport on foot before taking a wagon over the Allegheny Mountains. It rained incessantly during the trip, but Nichols still made the journey from Newport to Pittsburgh in four weeks.[44]

When he arrived in Danville, Jonathon got straight to work. He wrote to his brother William in April 1806 that he was "a bachelor placed in a wild country where time is pretty closely engaged in business and when at leisure more inclined to retirement...when he amuses himself sometimes with books."[45] Jonathon also expressed pride in the products he manufactured, writing his father about "sending samples of his work to a Rhode Island manufacturer."[46] He peppered his letters with details of his business dealings and the places where they shipped yarn and cordage.

In short time, Jonathon's hard work started to pay dividends, and he turned his attention to personal matters. He began courting Matilda Reed Ball, a young lady from one of Danville's leading families. Matilda Ball was the granddaughter of John Reed, who had settled in Danville in 1779. Reed, along with his neighbor Samuel Givens, established Givens-Reed Station, a fortified housing unit common on the Kentucky frontier. Jon and Matilda were married on November 20, 1808, in a "union (that) forever fixed the status of the engrafted Easterners."[47]

Ever mindful of opportunity, in June 1810, Nichols wrote his father, Walter, that he planned to open his own ropewalk.[48] Nichols's ropewalk was located on nine acres, with a business office, built around 1804, fronting the Wilderness Road. The factory was bounded by Lexington Pike to the north,

Office of Jonathon Nichols's ropewalk. The rope factory consumed most of the block behind this building.

Broadway to the south and First Street to the west. A well on the property supplied water for the entire factory.

From 1804 to 1810, Jonathan worked to develop relationships with a network of buyers and distributers from New Orleans to Rhode Island. Nichols also benefited from opening his ropewalk during the Napoleonic Wars (1803–15). In an effort to avoid becoming entangled in European conflicts, Congress passed the Embargo Act in 1807, which was replaced by the Non-Intercourse Act of 1809. Together, they "resulted in greater interest in Kentucky in the establishment of factories."[49]

The start of the War of 1812 further increased demand on domestic hemp producers. In 1813, Nichols wrote of sending forty tons of yarn to New York and Philadelphia, where it sold for ten cents per pound. He also shipped hemp downriver to New Orleans and overland by wagon into Pennsylvania.[50]

In 1814, Nichols wrote about how the war had impacted his business. The embargo that preceded the outbreak of the war interrupted supplies of imported hemp from Russia. This resulted in increased demand and higher prices for domestically produced hemp and hemp products. To meet rising demand and capitalize on good prices, more people began to speculate in the hemp industry either by growing hemp or starting hemp factories. More raw material and manufacturing competition drove prices down. While Nichols sold four hundred tons of hemp, he complained about business. He

Jonathon Nichols lived across the street from his ropewalk. He started a large house downtown but died before it was completed.

was still doing well enough to begin construction on a brick home for his family in downtown Danville.[51]

When Jonathon Nichols arrived, Danville was no longer considered the frontier. The locals did not consider him a pioneer. But Jonathon's industriousness quickly earned the respect of his established neighbors. He married into one of the early frontier families and thrived. He died in 1828, but he and his brother left an indelible imprint on Danville.

THE COMBS CENTER

Danville was one of Kentucky's leading hemp-producing regions into the twentieth century. And George Cogar was one of Danville's largest hemp merchants at the turn of the century. He is believed to be the first occupant when he moved his business into a new warehouse built on Walnut Street by the railroad tracks in 1902. By March 1905, George Cogar Hemp and Grain had already handled over 800,000 pounds of hemp through its warehouse.[52]

Top: "Breaking Hemp outside Danville, Kentucky." Published by McCurry & Sons in 1907. The postcard is labeled "Hemp Series, No. 7."

Bottom: Centre College's Combs Center occupies the warehouse building formerly owned by hemp dealer Banks Hudson. It operated into the 1940s.

Banks Hudson Sr. (1875–1953) acquired the warehouse in the 1920s.[53] He and his partner, J.C. Davis, made buying and selling hemp one of the staples of their business. They earned a reputation for offering top dollar and favorable terms to farmers and supplying high-quality hemp to their customers.[54]

In 1916, Hudson and Davis were part of the consortium—with David S. Gay, E.F. Spears and W.B. Nelson—collaborating on a proposal to supply 350 tons of hemp fiber to the U.S. Navy. The proposal was submitted by E.F. Spears and Sons to the navy on behalf of the group.[55]

The hemp industry in Kentucky had waned by the 1920s. In 1919, significantly better prices for burley tobacco and an acute labor shortage pushed hemp into the background of the state's agricultural landscape.[56] However, William Banks Hudson Sr. was one of the few Kentuckians who continued to grow, process and sell hemp through the 1930s and into the 1940s. He was awarded a significant contract with the navy in August 1940 worth $12,600.[57]

The former warehouse at 853 West Walnut Street is now owned by Centre College. Renamed the Combs Center, it is home to the college's offices for communications and leadership programs. The building has its original floors and beams, some of which bear the initials of workers long passed. The side of the building still bears a painted sign from its previous life.

3

HEMP IN BOURBON COUNTY

The first settlers into the Bourbon County area arrived in 1776. The area, located at the confluence of Stoner Creek and the South Fork of the Licking River, attracted early pioneers who named their community Hopewell. In 1785, Bourbon County was established as the fifth independent county in the Kentucky territory by the Virginia legislature.

Since its founding, Bourbon County has become renowned for its Thoroughbred horses and the distinctly American spirit named after it. But the county also has a rich hemp history whose roots entwine throughout the county narrative.

One of the chief hemp producing counties. Led production in 1810, accounting for 796 of the 5,755 tons grown in state. Two hemp mills processed 50,000 yards of fiber per year. After a slump during the Civil War, local farmers produced a crop of 569 tons in 1870. By 1900 production declined with a brief revival during the World Wars.[58]
—*Marker, US 68, Paris at William Alexander House*

Bourbon county was…named in compliment to the Bourbon family of France—a prince of that family, then upon the throne, having rendered the American colonies most important aid, in men and money, in the great struggle for independence.…It lies in the heart of the garden of Kentucky— the surface gently undulating, the soil remarkably rich and productive, based on Limestone with red clay foundation. Hemp, corn and wheat are cultivated in the county.

Paris, the principal town and county seat of Bourbon, is situated on the turnpike road from Maysville to Lexington, about forty-three miles from Frankfort. It is a neat and pleasant town, and is a place of considerable business and importance: Containing…three bagging factories.

The town was established by the Virginia legislature in 1780, under the name Hopewell, by which it was known for several years. It was also called Bourbonton, after the county in which it lies, but finally received its present name from the city of Paris in France.[59]

HEMP IN HOPEWELL

One reason that hemp became such an important crop so quickly was "its suitability for home manufacturers. The pioneers developed skill in manufacturing it as well as flax into cordage and cloth."[60] Kentucky's "homespun" industry generally produced textiles used for making clothes for enslaved people and agricultural workers, including items like "Kentucky jeans." However, spinning and weaving were not the only industries based around hemp culture. One of the earliest businesses in Hopewell was Adam M'Ferson's "blue diers business," which dyed threads made of cotton, flax and hemp as early as 1778.[61]

WILLIAM ALEXANDER

The federal style house was built for William W. Alexander, a state representative 1848–52. His father William Alexander owned a hemp factory until 1856, which was operated by 100 enslaved people. At 600 feet, it had one of the world's longest ropewalks. Hugh D. Alexander operated the house as a restaurant and saloon from the 1880's to 1908.[62]
—*Marker, US 68, East Paris, Kentucky*

Like many of the Bluegrass counties, Bourbon County had a flourishing hemp industry in the antebellum South. While the markets were far from stable, with boom-bust cycles occurring regularly, the hemp industry in central Kentucky generated huge amounts of wealth. After the War of 1812, from around 1815 to 1820, the market for hempen goods was so depressed that William Alexander "continued to manufacture a small quantity of baling materials, for which the only market was at Huntsville, Alabama."[63]

Alexander's business struggled with the postwar economic slump, but it did manage to survive. Kentuckians began to lobby their elected officials, and in the 1820s, Senator Henry Clay worked to enact the tariffs and protections that made up his "American System." By the 1840s, Kentucky's hemp industry had rebounded and was again thriving.

Another downturn occurred in the 1850s. Missouri now sat on the cusp of the frontier and had temporarily usurped Kentucky's place as the nation's leading hemp producer. In fact, many Kentuckians migrated to Missouri to pursue opportunities in the industry. William Alexander, perhaps feeling too old to weather another boom-bust cycle, quit the hemp industry in 1856 and died soon after.

THE SPEARS FAMILY

Jacob Spears (1754–1825) migrated to Kentucky from Pennsylvania in 1790, settling outside of Paris. Corn was a crop planted by Kentucky settlers in abundance to show "improvement" to land on which they were staking claim. Spears, like many settlers, realized that he needed to distill his corn into liquor in order to preserve its value and make it easier to transport to market. Along with his sons Noah and Solomon, Jacob Spears operated three distilleries in Bourbon County.

According to local legend, his son Solomon was one of several Kentucky pioneers with a claim on discovering bourbon whiskey. A fire at Solomon's warehouse resulted in several oaken barrels filled with corn liquor becoming charred. The alcohol's reaction to the charred wood turned the liquor brown and mellowed its bite, imparting a distinct flavor. This new spirit was eventually named "bourbon" and became wildly popular.[64]

Jacob's grandson Edward Ford "E.F." Spears (1840–1907) volunteered for the Confederacy during the Civil War. He joined the Second Kentucky Infantry, known as the Orphan's Brigade, and rose to the rank of captain. Following the war, E.F. worked as a grocer for two years before he partnered on a grain mill and distillery, Woodford, Spears & Clay. This partnership lasted nine years, then E.F. pivoted from distilling to focus on milling and other opportunities.[65]

In 1886, E.F. Spears acquired the coal, grain and seed business on Main Street in Paris formerly operated by his deceased brother William.[66] This was when E.F. started buying and selling hemp. In the early 1900s, Spears invested in the latest hemp-processing equipment from England. It was

Woodford Spears and Sons warehouse building, Main Street, Paris, Kentucky.

installed in a building just off the gravity mill, where it remains to this day. The processing line included a decorticator, a carding machine and a baler.

E.F. Spears died in 1907, and the business was inherited by his sons Woodford and Catesby. Renamed Woodford Spears and Sons in 1923, the firm continued to sell hemp until at least 1939 and successfully bid on government naval contracts into the 1930s. It also regularly prospected for new business with private cordage companies.[67]

Woodford Spears and Sons supplied raw hemp to one of the most publicized naval projects of the late 1920s. In July 1929, the company was notified that it had been awarded bid no. 1599 for seventy thousand pounds of grade B American hemp. The navy issued contract no. 13868 for hemp to be used "for manufacture of cordage for U.S. Frigate Constitution." At a purchase price of $0.1885 per pound, the contract was worth $13,195.00[68] Once restored, the *Constitution* functioned as a museum, complete with display cabinets and mannequins.

Through early 1939, correspondence between Spears and the Smith and Bird Company in New York discussed the price of Spears's remaining inventory. In April 1939, Woodford Spears had been offering the remainder of his hemp inventory for roughly $0.085 per pound. The response from Smith and Bird was that Wisconsin hemp was selling at $0.055–0.065 per pound.[69]

On September 1, 1939, Nazi Germany invaded Poland. France and England immediately declared war on Germany. On September 9, Spears received a telegram inquiring about his unsold inventory.[70] By October,

SAVE "OLD IRONSIDES"

Authorized by Act of Congress empowering the Secretary of the Navy to raise funds for this purpose

IX21/JJ21-(M).   CAP.

NATIONAL HEADQUARTERS
NAVY YARD, BOSTON, MASS.
Rear Admiral Philip Andrews, U. S. N., Chairman

JUL 3 - 1929

Woodford Spears & Sons,
Paris,
Kentucky.

Gentlemen:

      I have your letter of June 18th in regard to the availability of American hemp for the manufacture of cordage for the U. S. Frigate CONSTITUTION. I hope to be able to reach a decision within the next week or ten days as to just how we will go about acquiring the cordage for "Old Ironsides." In the meantime I would be pleased to be informed in case there is any change in the hemp situation.

      We have in mind to secure authority to purchase the raw material on local requisition so as to save the time incident to advertising from Washington. If we decide to make the rope at the Boston Navy Yard, rather than purchase the rope, we would want to get some deliveries of material within the next few months. In view of this I would be pleased to be informed what delivery dates could be satisfactorily met. The deliveries could be made in two or possibly three lots. Inasmuch as we have to specify delivery dates in making a contract we would be glad to hear from you on this point at an early date.

      Very truly yours,

Philip Andrews,
Rear Admiral, U.S.Navy.

THE U. S. FRIGATE CONSTITUTION
LAUNCHED 1797

NATIONAL EXECUTIVE COMMITTEE

PHILIP ANDREWS
REAR ADMIRAL. U. S. N
CURTIS D. WILBUR
SECRETARY OF THE NAVY
T. DOUGLAS ROBINSON
ASSISTANT SECRETARY OF THE NAVY
LOUIS R. DE STEIGUER
REAR ADMIRAL, U. S. N.
A. C. RATSHESKY
PRESIDENT U. S. TRUST CO., BOSTON, TREAS.
L. M. JOSEPHTHAL
REAR ADMIRAL, N.Y. NAVAL MILITIA
MRS. SAMUEL PRESTON DAVIS
PRESIDENT NATIONAL SOCIETY UNITED STATES DAUGHTERS OF 1812
JAMES R. NICHOLSON
PAST GRAND EXALTED RULER, B. P. O. E

NATIONAL COMMITTEE

HON. FRANK B. KELLOGG
SECRETARY OF STATE
HON. WILLIAM M. JARDINE
SECRETARY OF AGRICULTURE
HON. HERBERT HOOVER
FORMER SECRETARY OF COMMERCE
HON. JAMES J. DAVIS
SECRETARY OF LABOR
HON. HANFORD MACNIDER
ASST. SECRETARY OF WAR
HON. FREDERICK HALE
U. S. SENATOR FROM MAINE
HON. BURTON L. FRENCH
MEMBER OF CONGRESS FROM IDAHO
E. W. EBERLE
ADMIRAL U. S. N.
CHARLES P. SUMMERALL
MAJOR GEN. U. S. A.
J. L. HINES
MAJOR GEN. U. S. A
F. C. BILLARD
REAR ADMIRAL U. S. C. G.
HON. FRANKLIN D. ROOSEVELT
FORMER ASST. SECRETARY OF THE NAVY
ROGER K. ROGAN
CINCINNATI, OHIO

FINANCE COMMITTEE

ALLAN FORBES
PRESIDENT STATE STREET TRUST
CHARLES E. COTTING
LEE, HIGGINSON & CO.
JOHN R. MACOMBER
PRESIDENT, HARRIS, FORBES & CO.
JAMES J. PHELAN
HORNBLOWER & WEEKS
PHILIP ANDREWS
REAR ADMIRAL, U. S. N.
A. C. RATSHESKY
PRESIDENT UNITED STATES TRUST CO.
L. M. JOSEPHTHAL
REAR ADMIRAL, N.Y. NAVAL MILITIA

England, thru popular subscription, saved Lord Nelson's flagship the Victory, for all time. Can we do less with our immortal vessel the Constitution?

"Old Ironsides" saved the Nation; now let us save Her

Award notification to Woodford Spears and Sons for hemp contract for the "Save Old Ironsides" project.

a contract for all of Spears's remaining hemp had been signed. The materials, worth $2,902.76, shipped to the Columbian Rope Company in Auburn, New York. That November, Spears wrote, "This cleans us out of all grades of hemp."[71]

Spears and Bird continued to correspond. In early December, Smith wrote, "If the war continues, it would be advisable to put in a big crop of Kentucky hemp," mentioning a British buyer who sought to purchase five hundred tons of hemp.[72] Spears responded, "There is so little hemp seed to be had in Kentucky we fear now it will be most difficult to get any size crop of fiber another year. If the war keeps up, we believe next Spring seed could be planted and the following year hemp could be grown from it in quantities."[73] Based on Spears's timeline, if Kentucky producers implemented their plan immediately, a seed crop in 1940 would produce a fiber crop in 1941. That fiber would have been available in the winter/spring of 1942.

In the winter of 2020, the Spears family donated their family papers documenting their hemp business to the University of Kentucky Special Collections Library. The records date from the late 1890s to 1939. No records have yet been discovered that indicate they contributed to the war effort from 1941 to 1945.[74]

The Courthouse Rotunda

At the turn of the twentieth century, hemp was still Kentucky's leading cash crop and vital to the state's economy. In Bourbon County, hemp received an amazing artistic tribute. In 1906, the county dedicated a new courthouse

Hemp breaking represents the agricultural activity during winter in the rotunda mural of the Bourbon County Courthouse in Paris, Kentucky, built in 1905.

building. Designed by Frank P. Millburn, the beaux arts structure features a rotunda painted with murals depicting "Bourbon County's great agricultural story."[75] Agricultural activity during each season is depicted. The winter portion of the mural depicts Black laborers breaking hemp in the field. Construction on the building started in 1903 and finished in 1905 at a cost of $170,000. This incredible work of art memorializes Kentucky's hemp industry for the ages.

4

CLARK COUNTY HEMP

Hemp for Victory

One of the ten Bluegrass counties which produced over 90 percent of the entire countries yield in late 1800's. Production increased from 155 tons in 1869 to over 1,000 tons in 1889, valued at about $125 per ton. In 1942, Winchester selected as site of one of 42 cordage plants built throughout the country to offset fiber shortage during war.[76]
—Marker 1319, US 60 West, outside the Stuff Recycling and Scrap

Clark County's hempstory touches several significant historical eras. While the sign alludes to hemp in the late 1800s and during the Second World War, the story starts with the first pioneers.

The earliest record of hemp in Clark County appears in a journal entry from William Clinkenbeard in 1779. It illustrates the role hemp played in the pioneer homestead. The former resident of Strode's Station wrote: "The first hemp seed I got was while I was in the station after I was married. Saved the stalks and broke it up and my wife made me a shirt out of it."[77]

In 1792, one of the first acts of the newly created Kentucky legislature was to establish three hemp inspection stations. One of these inspection stations was at the warehouses located at Holder's Landing, an industrial site on Lower Howard's Creek.[78] Parts of the site are protected from development within the John Holder Nature Conservancy. The entire area was one of Kentucky's first industrial sites and included warehousing and boatyard facilities. Outside of the inspection warehouse, there is no evidence of hemp being processed into manufactured goods. There is a trail within the conservancy, for reserved tours only, that winds up the creek bed past the remains of several early settlement buildings.

> *Clark county was the fourteenth county in Kentucky, created out of parts of Fayette and Bourbon counties in 1792.*[79] *It was named in honor of General George Rogers Clark and situated in the middle section of the state....Half of the western half of Clark county is very productive, the soil being as good as any in Kentucky.*
>
> *The exports consist principally of hemp, cattle, horses, mules, and hogs.*
>
> *Winchester is the county seat, situated on the Lexington and Mount Sterling Road....It contains...two hemp factories.*[80]

Hemp Manufacturing in Antebellum Winchester

In his ongoing research into Clark County history, Harry Enoch identified the owners and locations of both of Winchester's antebellum hemp factories.

David Dodge (1771–1819) started Winchester's first hemp-manufacturing facility in 1811. Dodge moved to Lexington, Kentucky, from New York in 1797, where he initially partnered with Thomas Hart on a ropewalk. In 1809, Dodge expressed his intent to start his own business. This culminated with Dodge moving to Winchester to open a ropewalk and bagging factory. The intersection of Main and Hickman Streets formed the northwest boundary of the property. The manufacturing center was located on a lot that today includes the Bluegrass Heritage Museum. Dodge initially did well and, among other speculative ventures, opened a ropewalk in Mount Sterling. By 1815, Dodge was overextended and started to mortgage his holdings. His home and the factory in Winchester were mortgaged in 1818.

In 1819, James Morrison of Lexington purchased the factory from Dodge's trustee. Morrison, a wealthy ropewalk owner in Lexington, operated the Winchester factory until his death in 1823. Morrison left his daughter Hettie Morrison Hawes $10,000 worth of property that she used to acquire the ropewalk and bagging factory. She and her husband, attorney Richard Hawes, moved to Winchester in 1824 and operated the factory for several years. They formed a partnership with Benjamin Buckner, to whom they later sold the factory in 1833.

At its peak, the Buckner factory "worked 60 hands." These "hands" were likely enslaved people. An apparent disagreement between Hawes and Buckner resulted in a lawsuit, decided in October 1842. The court decision resulted in the factory being put up for auction, selling for $2,500. Fauntleroy Jones, who would later become one of Kentucky's leading horticulturists, bought the factory but never attempted to operate it. He and his wife sold "all the buildings and improvements" to Dr. Warren Frazier for $2,400. There are no records of the factory operating after 1842.

Robert J. Didlake and David P. Bullock attempted to capitalize on a relatively hot market for hemp when they opened their hemp factory in 1848. At its peak, the factory "worked 40 hands," most likely enslaved people. But by 1850, the hemp industry in Kentucky was entering one of its frequent bust periods. Competition from Missouri threatened to supplant Kentucky as the center of the nation's hemp industry. In 1850, Didlake bought out Bullock. But by 1851, Didlake wanted out and sold to A.M. Keith and C.T. Haggard for $1,000. Haggard and Keith operated the factory for several years before selling it to James Levi Wheeler for $281 in 1854.[81]

As the 1850s progressed, hemp was not as prominent to the Kentucky economy as it had been. As new supply chains developed to feed domestic markets and compete with Kentucky manufacturers and producers, the amount of hemp grown and factories manufacturing it into products decreased.

RAILROADS AND THE WAREHOUSE ERA

Following the Civil War, the hemp industry in Clark County was relatively dormant until the railroad came to Winchester. The first rail line to reach Winchester was the Elizabethtown, Lexington and Big Sandy in 1873. By 1881, that line extended as far as Catletsburg, where it linked with the Chesapeake and Ohio Railroad. For the first time, Winchester was directly linked to markets in the East. By 1889, seven rail lines converged in Winchester.[82]

VALENTINE WHITE BUSH: WINCHESTER'S FIRST RAIL SIDE WAREHOUSE

Anticipating the access to markets that the railroad would provide, Valentine White Bush (1831–1899) constructed the first warehouse along the proposed route in 1880. Shortly after opening the warehouse, Bush advertised that he would purchase "hemp, wheat and other grains."[83] The

This is the first of Winchester, Kentucky's rail-side warehouses, Vaughn Warehouse (aka Sphar Seed). It collapsed in 2019 despite efforts to save it.

warehouse site also included a "hackling house" for cleaning hemp before it was put into storage. Sanborn maps indicate that V.W. Bush operated the warehouse until he died in 1900, when his third wife, Kate, inherited the business and ran it until at least 1912. The warehouse last insured a hackling house around 1895, by which time Bush had apparently ceded warehousing hemp fiber to the competition.

The business changed hands several times: "V.W. Bush, Goff & Bush, Sphar & Co and Sphar Feed & Seed."[84] It closed for good in 2005. Parts of the building had been neglected for years prior to its closing. The City of Winchester acquired title to the property in 2016 with hopes of making restoration efforts the cornerstone of "revitalizing the North Winchester area."[85] However, restoration efforts stalled, and in 2020, parts of the building collapsed.

The warehouse model Bush established was an economic epiphany for Clark County that transformed Winchester. The warehouse operator functioned as a vital middleman and broker for agricultural produce.[86] The railroad-adjacent warehouse became the place where farmers and other producers could sell their crops in bulk at an advertised price. It saved them the time and expense of finding buyers for each crop. For buyers, the warehouse created a one-stop market for agricultural commodities. Buyers purchased hemp, tobacco, grain and seed in bulk.

David S. Gay Puts Winchester Hemp on the Map

David S. Gay (1864–1923) utilized this business model to transform Winchester into a hub of hemp commerce. From the 1890s until the early 1920s, David Gay was one of the nation's leading hemp merchants. Gay and his partner, W.M. Jones, built a hackling house and warehouse on North Main Street near the railroad depot, across the street from V.W. Bush, in 1886.[87]

By 1895, Gay was operating the warehouse on his own and was incredibly successful. In the early 1900s, he bid on contracts for hemp fiber from the Boston Naval Shipyard. In 1901, he outbid several other Kentucky hemp merchants to secure a contract for 125 tons of American hemp worth $26,250.[88] And in 1903, he secured a contract for 150 tons of American hemp worth $42,840.[89] By 1907, Gay's warehousing empire in Winchester encompassed three locations and included grain and bluegrass seed. But David S. Gay's reputation was built out of hemp.

By 1916, Gay was widely known as "one of the largest hemp dealers in the nation,"[90] and because of his efforts, Winchester was regarded as "the largest domestic hemp market in the United States."[91] Correspondence on display at the Bluegrass Heritage Museum among Gay, E.F. Spears and two

The September 1916 agreement among Hudson Banks, E.F. Spears, David Gay and W.B. Nelson for a joint bid on a U.S. Navy hemp contract. On display at the Bluegrass Heritage Museum.

other area hemp merchants reveals that they worked together on a bid for the Boston Naval Yard for 350 tons of hemp.

World War I was Winchester's hemp industry's last hurrah for a long time. David Gay died in 1923, and with him, so did Winchester's hemp industry. Growers may have been able to find buyers in neighboring Paris or Lexington, but by 1929, no hemp was reported grown in Clark County.[92]

HEMP FOR VICTORY

The domestic hemp industry was almost nonexistent in the 1930s. By 1937, hemp's relationship and physical resemblance to "marihuana" had created a crippling legal environment for the industry. The Marihuana Tax Act of 1937 was the result of a public awareness campaign about the use of the cannabis plant as a recreational drug. The language of the tax on the transfer of hemp from grower to mill owner created an insurmountable financial obstacle. By 1939, four farms in Kentucky grew a total of ninety tons of hemp fiber; another six farms grew thirty acres of seed hemp. The three cord and twine factories still in operation mostly processed imported fibers like sisal.[93]

Concurrent with the surprise attack on Pearl Harbor in 1941, Japan also invaded the Philippine Islands, cutting off the U.S. Navy's supply of marine fiber. Since the conclusion of the Spanish-American War in 1898, a large portion of the navy's fiber requirements was met with abaca, a fiber plant from the banana family, also known as "Manila Hemp." The interruption of this supply of marine-quality fiber, combined with the rising demands for cordage and other hemp products by the warring European nations, threatened to create a shortage of this vital war material.[94] While metal anchor chains and cords of twisted steel had come to replace most of the hemp rope used to rig ships, hemp rope was still used to load and secure cargo and for bow and stern lines tying ships to docks.

At the onset of American entry into the war, it appeared as if an emergency program to secure hemp fiber was a priority. In early 1942, the War Department established the Commodity Credit Corporation to help secure a domestic supply of hemp and other war materials. The "Hemp for Victory" program, as it's now called, was established to ensure the supply of hemp fiber. The U.S. Department of Agriculture initiated a program to train farmers and establish a network of hemp mills to process the hemp stalks into fiber. To support this program, the USDA issued *Farmers Bulletin*

1935, "Hemp,"[95] and produced a promotional film, *Hemp for Victory*, to raise awareness.

And it was not just the navy that required hemp to function. Hemp blend thread was used for a variety of applications for all branches of the military. Among the many applications for hemp mentioned in the film were the following: "rope for marine rigging and towing; for hay forks, derricks and heavy-duty tackle; light duty firehose; thread for shoes for millions of American soldiers; and parachute webbing for our paratroopers."[96]

Kentucky's role in the hemp industry had changed radically since its heyday in the 1840s. Kentucky hemp fiber farmers had not embraced available technology, and hemp fiber production gradually shifted to the Midwest. As fiber production migrated out of state, Kentucky farmers focused on producing hemp seed. Kentucky seed was ideally suited for fiber production farther north. Hemp from Kentucky seed grew tall and thin, resulting in ideal fibers. The shorter growing season at northern latitudes also meant that the hemp was generally ready for harvest before seeds ripened.

The "Hemp for Victory" program built forty-two hemp mills during the war, only one of which was located in Kentucky, the mill in Winchester.[97] It

Guarding the strategic reserve of hemp seed during World War II, Lexington, Kentucky. 1942. *National Archives file 94533220.*

was located on US 60 West just inside the Fayette/Clark County border, and construction commenced in the spring of 1943.

Wisconsin's leading hemp agronomist, Andrew Wright, is believed to have contributed to the design. The concept maximized the flow of materials. Hemp was delivered at one end of the mill, where it entered the dryer. Next, it went through the decorticating and carding processes. The decorticating machine eliminated the intense labor of breaking hemp, while carding softened the fiber. The mills were designed to be relatively self-sufficient. Hemp hurds, rich in cellulose, powered the dryers and warmed the mills.[98]

The Winchester mill operated only one season, processing one crop. By 1944, the tide of World War II had turned and several traditional sources of fiber had been restored. Most of the hemp processed into fiber during the war was never actually consumed. A significant portion of the domestic hemp fiber produced made up a strategic reserve. Of this, a large portion was improperly stored and destroyed. Contrary to popular belief, Hemp for Victory did not make a significant contribution to the war effort and was basically a "$30 Million insurance policy."[99]

Hemp for Victory was terminated at the end of the war, and the mills were sold as government surplus. The mill in Winchester was sold by the government in 1948 and converted into an aluminum siding factory.[100] Later, it was used as a lumberyard and eventually a recycling center. After years of neglect, the building was eventually torn down in 2017.

The Historic Log Cabin bed-and-breakfast at Mount Folly Farm, Winchester, Kentucky.

Winchester is also home to several businesses involved in Kentucky's modern hemp revival. The most historic and tourist-friendly of these businesses is Mount Folly Farm, creators of Laura's Homestead Alternative brand of CBD products. Founded by organic food pioneer Laura Freeman, the brand utilizes CO_2 to extract CBD from their organically raised hemp. The hemp farm features a two-story log cabin built in 1792 and recently renovated into a "pioneer homestead"–themed bed-and-breakfast, complete with modern amenities. The farm hosts several celebrations and educational events during the year, with topics including hemp cultivation, sustainable agriculture and environmental protection.

5

FAYETTE COUNTY HEMP

Center of the Hempire

The two hemp-related historical markers in Fayette County share a familial connection. The "Fayette County Hemp" sign, one of the state's missing markers, mentions John Wesley Hunt, who opened the first hemp bagging factory in the United States in 1803. The other marker memorializes his grandson, Confederate general John Hunt Morgan, who operated a successful hemp factory in Lexington prior to joining the Confederate army.

Fayette county was formed in 1780 by the State of Virginia, and was one of the three original counties that at one time comprised the whole district of Kentucky and received its name as a testimonial of gratitude to Gen. Gilbert Mortier De La Fayette—the gallant and generous Frenchman who volunteered as the Champion of Liberty....

Fayette county is located in the center of the garden of Kentucky...the soil is probably as rich and productive as any upon which the sun ever shone. It is properly a stock raising county...but corn and hemp are produced in great abundance—the latter being generally manufactured in the county.

The manufacture of hemp is carried on very extensively in Lexington and the county of Fayette. In the city there are 15 hemp establishments, working six hundred hands, running 90 looms, and making annually 2,500,000 pounds of rope. In the suburbs of the city there are four factories, manufacturing 680,000 yards of bagging and 400,000 pounds of rope. In the remainder of the county there are fourteen factories, working three hundred hands, running 50 looms, and turning out 1,250,000 yards bagging, 1,000,000 pounds of rope. Thus, in the city and county there are thirty-three bagging and rope establishments, working one thousand fifty hands, running one hundred and sixty-five looms, and making 4,430,000 yards of bagging and 2,400,000 pounds of rope.[101]

Raising and processing hemp was one of the first industries established on the frontier. The area that would become Fayette County developed into a hub of hemp industrialism filled with mills, ropewalks and bagging factories. The first ropewalk in Lexington was opened by John Hamilton in 1790.[102] He was followed by many others, transforming Lexington into the center of Kentucky's "hempire."

The hemp industry literally transformed Lexington into the light of the frontier. Not only did Lexington lead the state in hemp manufacturing, but the town's first streetlights were also likely fueled by hemp seed oil. Lexington was the first "western town" with street lamps; as many as twenty street lamps were installed by 1812. With such a high volume of hemp being processed, hemp seed oil would have been a logical choice to fuel street lamps. Hemp oil has a short shelf life as far as food use. However, "compared with other oils, hemp oil produces a very bright light in a lamp, perhaps because of its higher ignition point."[103]

WAVELAND: A BOONE FAMILY STORY

Kentucky history and folklore is rich with the exploits of the state's first explorers and frontiersmen. Perhaps the most famous is Daniel Boone. Before it was opened to settlement, Boone explored the Kentucky territory several times. In 1767–68, he explored the eastern mesa and Big Sandy River on a "hunting expedition" that left him unimpressed. He returned to Kentucky in May 1769 with John Findley, a former scout from Fort Duquesne in Pittsburgh with whom Boone had served during the French and Indian War. Findley led Boone and four other men on a hunting expedition deep into territory he had previously scouted. As the party headed back to North Carolina, they encountered another hunting party entering Kentucky led by Daniel's brother Squire Boone Jr. Daniel decided to remain in Kentucky with his brother. The Boone brothers did not return to their families until 1771.[104]

Squire Boone Sr. (1696–1765), Daniel's father, moved the Boone family from Pennsylvania to the Yadkin River valley of North Carolina in 1750.[105] They settled near the farm of Captain Morgan Bryan (1671–1763), who had moved there with his family from Virginia in 1748.[106] The two families became very close and saw several marriages.

The two families attempted to homestead in the newly opened Kentucky Territory in September 1773. Their party attempted to enter Kentucky through the Cumberland Gap, but they returned to North Carolina after six members of the group, including Daniel's oldest son, James, were attacked and killed by Indians. Following this and other Indian attacks on settlers and surveyors throughout 1774, Boone was recruited by Virginia governor Lord Dunmore to warn other settlers and surveyors about hostile Indians.[107]

The campaign against the Indians, called "Dunmore's War," concluded with the Indian defeat at the Battle of Point Pleasant on October 10, 1774. After the campaign, the Boones and Bryans made another attempt to settle Kentucky. In 1775, Boone was hired by Judge Henderson and the Transylvania Company to organize a team of thirty ax men to blaze an overland route into Kentucky through the Cumberland Gap. The trail was named the "Wilderness Road."[108] Boone led a party to the Kentucky River and began construction of Fort Boonesborough in what is now Madison County.

At the outbreak of the Revolutionary War, many Indian tribes in Ohio allied themselves with the British. The Indians were upset that their defeat by Lord Dunmore had cost them the rights to hunting grounds in Kentucky. They hoped that a British victory in the war would evict the settlers and restore their hunting rights. As attacks along the frontier increased, Boonesborough was attacked several times.

In 1779, Daniel Boone's father-in-law Joseph Bryan and his three brothers, Morgan, James and William, established Bryan's Station along the North Fork of Elkhorn Creek in Fayette County, five miles northeast of Lexington. The station was well fortified and featured "forty-four log cabins arranged in a 200 by 50-yard compound that was surrounded by a 12-foot-high stockade and included a two-story blockhouse." The water supply was located outside the stockade, a glaring weakness in an otherwise stout fortification.[109] In May 1780, William Bryan was killed by Indians while leading a hunting expedition.[110]

THE SIEGE OF BRYAN'S STATION

In the summer of 1782 a force of British Loyalists, including a regiment known as Butler's Rangers, and allied Indians comprising Shawnee, Delaware and Huron warriors mounted their largest Kentucky operation of the Revolutionary War. A force reportedly comprising between five hundred and six hundred Indians, including "famed renegade Simon Girty," hoped to surprise the settlers at Bryan's Station. They planned to sneak up on the station and attack the garrison in the morning, when the gates to the stockade were opened. But the settlers were aware of the presence of the Indians. Not wanting to arouse the Indians' suspicion, a group of women, led by Jemima Suggett Johnson (1753–1814), made their morning trek to the spring for water. After the women return to the station, the men sprang a small trap on the Indians, luring them into attacking the fort when the Indians thought it was empty.

The Siege of Bryan's Station lasted from August 14 until the morning of August 16. The British and Indians believed their superior numbers would be enough to intimidate the defenders. During the siege, "the renegade Simon Girty approached the fort through a field in which the hemp, high as a man's head, concealed him from the eyes of the besieged marksman."[111] Girty demanded the station's surrender, then overplayed his hand and bluffed about the arrival of reinforcements and artillery. The garrison was not impressed. One of the settlers responded that he had a dog named Simon Girty and that the entire countryside was now headed toward the station's rescue. Unnerved, the Indians hastily withdrew on the morning of August 16. Scouts sent out by the fort reported finding cookfires still burning and food in the process of preparation.[112]

The British commander, Captain William Caldwell (1750–1822), had a different perspective on the siege and the follow-up engagement, the Battle of Blue Licks. In his report of August 26, 1782, Caldwell claimed he was marching to Wheeling in the Virginia colony when he was intercepted by a party of Shawnee who claimed to have information about nearby enemy activity. A small skiff had come up the Licking River and landed several men. The Indians assumed it was General George Rogers Clark and immediately sent word to Caldwell.[113]

Caldwell claimed to have over 1,100 Indian warriors assembled to confront Clark. When the report proved false, Caldwell claimed that most of the assembled Indians returned home.

Undaunted, Caldwell crossed the Ohio River "determined to pay the enemy a visit with as many Indians as would follow." He wrote that his combined force of "three hundred Indians and Rangers...marched for Bryant's Station on Kentuck." As the siege unfolded, Caldwell claimed that his initial plan to take a prisoner failed because "the Indians were in too great a hurry." Ultimately, he claimed his force "kill'd 300 hogs, 150 head of cattle, and a number of sheep, took a number of horses, pull'd up and destroyed their potatoes, cut down a great deal of their corn, burnt their *hemp*, and did other considerable damage" before retreating from the fort. Caldwell's force withdrew north, where it ambushed the pursuing Kentuckians at the Battle of Blue Licks.[114]

BUILDING A HEMP PLANTATION

In 1786, Daniel Boone Bryan (1758–1845), Daniel's nephew, established a plantation south of Lexington that became known as Waveland. The estate originally encompassed two thousand acres surveyed by Daniel Boone for his namesake nephew. When Daniel Boone Bryan died in 1845, Waveland included a blacksmith shop, a gunsmith shop, a gunpowder mill, a distillery, a gristmill, a paper mill, a female seminary and a

Waveland State Historical Home, home of Daniel Boone Bryan, Lexington, Kentucky. It was named for fields of hemp waving in the breeze surrounding the estate.

Slave quarters at Waveland State Historical Home, Lexington, Kentucky.

Baptist church.[115] "Waveland exemplify[ied] plantation life in Kentucky in the 19th-century; from the acres of grain and hemp waving in the breeze [hence the Waveland name], to the raising and racing of blooded trotting horses."[116]

Daniel's son Joseph Bryan inherited the plantation in 1845 and immediately set about replacing his father's original stone house with a Greek Revival mansion.

Like most plantations of this period, Waveland exploited the labor of enslaved people. Over the decades, the number of people enslaved at Waveland rose steadily. In the early 1830s, records reveal that six people were enslaved at Waveland. By 1848, that number had risen to nineteen. The Bryan family as a whole enslaved a total of sixty-seven people in 1860. For large agricultural projects, enslaved people would be hired or rented, often from an adjoining farm.[117]

The property was acquired by the Commonwealth of Kentucky in 1971 and converted into a museum. Along with the restored Greek Revival antebellum home, the property also includes three original outbuildings: the smokehouse, the icehouse and the living quarters for enslaved people.[118] The museum focuses on re-creating what antebellum life was like at the home in the 1850s.

Eli Cleveland's Industrial Site on Boone Creek

On February 6, 1793, Eli Cleveland advertised his hemp mill on Boone Creek in southern Fayette County in the *Kentucky Gazette*, the first newspaper west of the Allegheny Mountains.

> *The subscriber informs his friends, and the public that his hemp mill lately built is now in compleat* [sic] *order, and ready to take in hemp for the purpose of milling the same; to be well done and fit for the hackle, for one eighth part of the quantity brought to the mill. One bed is 120 lbs, and can be delivered in one hour and an* [sic] *half the same is put; one wagon* [sic] *load can be done in two days. Those who may favor the said mill with their custom, will find their business executed with care and dispatch, by Eli Cleveland N. B. Hemp not to be brought twisted.*[119]

The mill complex, which also included a gristmill and sawmill, was part of a larger industrial site that included warehousing and a boatyard near the Kentucky River.

Eli Cleveland makes an earlier appearance in the Kentucky narrative. In June 1786, General George Rogers Clark proposed military action against raiding Indian tribes. The call was echoed by Virginia governor Patrick Henry, whose brother had recently been killed in a battle with Indians.

Ruins of Eli Cleveland's mill complex at Boone Creek Outdoors, Lexington, Kentucky. In 1896, the *Kentucky Gazetter* reported that Cleveland's mill was vandalized.

Congress refused the request, hoping to avoid war. It was not a popular decision with local officials. "They creatively misconstrued official directives, connived with sympathetic army officers, and used their formal authority to dragoon men."[120] Governor Henry attempted to thread a political needle. He "noted that the Articles of Confederation permitted militia to attack preemptively if they 'received certain advice' of imminent invasion" and "implied they could exploit the loophole to justify the campaign." Local leaders submitted a "legal opinion" which "three Kentucky magistrates ruled that the "governor's message empowered militia officers to draft men and impress supplies."[121]

Many settlers opposed these measures. This included "Eli Cleveland, an aged Fayette County magistrate, [who] publicly denied the plans legality, ridiculed its promoters, and threatened to kill anyone who tried to impress his property." His statements emboldened other settlers, some of whom "forcibly reclaimed requisitioned cattle." In response, Levi Todd, commander of the militia, "ordered half a dozen men to seize Cleveland's 'Beef, Bacon and pack horses' and kill the old man if he resisted."[122]

When the militia arrived, Cleveland's wife, Mary, "blocked the farm gate." Todd's militia responded violently. They tore down Cleveland's fence and drove off his livestock, while conscripts held Mary at gunpoint. Todd then had Eli arrested and "stripped of his officer's commission." Todd even petitioned the governor to annul Cleveland's position as magistrate.[123]

For all the bravery Todd's militia may have shown at Cleveland's farm, its effectiveness during General George Rogers Clark's military campaign is more questionable. Clark marched the militia "several hundred miles in the September heat." The militia members, worn out and at the end of their rations, missed home. While bivouacked near the Vermillion River, one of the men reportedly shouted, "Who's for home?" In response, most of the regiment "turn'd back in Full Disorder." Clark attempted to get ahead of the impending military disaster by occupying the town of Vincennes and forcing nearby Indians, already peaceful, into the Treaty of Vincennes. Not long after this, Clark's superiors stripped him of "both his military command and his post as congressional Indian commissioner."[124]

Perhaps this episode foreshadows difficulties Cleveland encountered later operating his mill. In a letter to the *Kentucky Gazette* of March 28, 1796, Cleveland wrote, "My mills were burnt last night, and most confidently have been done by some of my enemies." Cleveland was certain the fire was set in malice, "as I have received private injuries of that kind, &c., before, and their malice is still raging."

Cleveland's industrial complex included grist-, hemp and sawmills, warehousing and a boatyard near Lexington, Kentucky.

The author enjoys the zipline view of Cleveland's Mill at Boone Creek Outdoors, Lexington, Kentucky. *Courtesy Boone Creek Outdoors.*

On April 4, 1796, Cleveland followed up with another letter, apparently in an attempt to dispel some viscous rumors.

Whereas there are divers reports propagated by my enemies, concerning the burning of my mills—it appears from their behavior and language, that they would willingly make the public believe, that some innocent person was the cause, and have gone as far to say I burnt them myself, which reports are intended to cloak their own villany.[125]

One June 22, 1796, Cleveland officially listed his industrial site for sale in the *Kentucky Gazette*. The mills came with four hundred acres of land, his ferry, boatyard and orchards. For whatever reason, the mills did not sell immediately. But by 1801, Jeremiah and Joseph Rogers had purchased the property and renamed it "Roger's Mill."[126]

Today, the natural beauty of the gorge and the archaeological remains of Eli Cleveland's hemp mill are home to a different type of business. A large section of the original site has been converted by Boone Creek Outdoors into the high adventure of a zip line canopy tour. The adventure features six zip lines, three sky bridges and several other places where guests get a bird's-eye view of the scenic gorge. A two-mile hiking tour that explores the mill remains is also offered.

JOHN WESLEY HUNT: THE MAN ON THE MARKER

Consistently the leader in hemp production and cordage making in Kentucky. In 1803, Hunt and Brand Co. produced the first hemp bagging made in the U.S. In the early 1840's the county had 63 ropewalks; they were long, narrow sheds for spiral winding of hemp fibers. In 1871, 2,000 tons of fiber were harvested, 1/3 yield for the entire state in that year.[127]
—Marker 1163, intersection Newtown Pike 922
and Ironworks Pike 1973, sign missing

Previously located at the intersection of Ironworks Pike and Newtown Pike, near an old hemp warehouse, this marker introduces one of Lexington's most prominent citizens, John Wesley Hunt. Born in Trenton, New Jersey, in 1773, John was ambitious to make his mark in the business world at an early age. By the time he was nineteen, Hunt had already impulsively pursued several different business opportunities.[128]

Civil War–era hemp warehouse at the intersection of Newtown Pike and Iron Works Pike, Lexington, Kentucky. It was built from brick to prevent fire.

John learned from his experiences, becoming more patient in his decisions and persistent in his follow-through. His cousin Abijah Hunt noticed John's maturation and approached him with a business opportunity. Abijah ran a successful general store in Cincinnati and wanted to expand his business by opening a store in Lexington. He offered John a partnership, and John jumped at the opportunity, moving to Lexington in 1795. John quickly established himself as a successful "pioneer merchant."[129]

Pioneer merchants like John and Abijah bought goods from merchants and wholesalers in the East and had them delivered to Pittsburgh. In Pittsburgh, they hired boats and floated the goods down the Ohio River to ports in Kentucky, usually Limestone (Maysville). From Maysville, goods were hauled overland to John's store on Main Street in Lexington.

Settlement in Kentucky boomed after the Revolutionary War. The Indian tribes allied with the British during the war had already surrendered their right to hunt in Kentucky after Dunmore's War in 1774. Their alliance with the British during the revolution weakened them even further. Raiding parties seldom ventured beyond the settlements along the south bank of the Ohio River. As the fear of Indians subsided, the flow of settlers increased. The general store provided these settlers with the goods and tools to tame the frontier.

Conversely, as settlers started to generate a surplus of agricultural goods, general stores became markets where they traded or sold their excess produce.

Initially, the Hunts took the products they acquired in whiskey, bacon, animal hides and furs, tobacco and hemp and floated them downriver to markets in Natchez and New Orleans. Once these goods were sold, John returned to Philadelphia. He paid any outstanding debts that were owed and secured more goods to take to Kentucky, where the cycle was repeated.

Abijah had developed a solid network of business contacts. This included merchants, wholesalers and financiers in Philadelphia from whom they purchased their goods, as well as merchants and buyers in places like Natchez and New Orleans to whom they sold Kentucky goods. John established a solid reputation as a trustworthy, intelligent businessman, developing strong relationships with all of Abijah's contacts.

In 1793, Eli Whitney patented the cotton gin, sparking a boom in the cotton industry of the Deep South. In July 1801, John Hunt wrote his father about his interest in the emerging hemp industry. That December, he followed up with a letter to his cousin Abijah, asking his opinion about opportunities in the hemp industry. Abijah replied that hemp bagging and cordage, used to bale cotton, would likely sell well. It was estimated that each three-hundred-pound bale of cotton required approximately fifteen pounds of hemp bagging and cordage.[130] He and John determined that bagging produced in Kentucky and floated downriver to Natchez could be sold at a cheaper price and at a greater margin than bagging materials imported from Europe. Abijah provided the specifications and ordered 6,000 yards of bagging materials from his cousin John. Abijah stipulated that should John's baling materials prove comparable in quality to European product, he would contract for 15,000 to 20,000 yards the following year. Henry Turner, a commission merchant in Natchez, was equally interested at the prospect of purchasing hemp bagging from Hunt's factory. Turner had imported 25,000 yards of hemp bagging from England the previous year. He was certain that domestic product could be sourced at a better price.[131]

Around the time his travels sparked Hunt's interest in hemp manufacturing, he also observed that there was a shortage of enslaved people on the plantations of the Deep South. In response, Hunt helped create the interstate traffic in enslaved people. For a number of reasons, Kentucky had more enslaved people than labor demands required. In 1800 and 1801, John and his cousins Abijah, Jeremiah and Jesse Hunt began to purchase enslaved people from farmers in Fayette County to sell to the cotton and sugar plantations in Mississippi.[132] When the federal government banned the importation of enslaved people starting in 1808, Kentucky's interstate traffic in enslaved people exploded.

Hunt then put together a plan for his hemp business. Making use of the contacts and relationships he built early in his partnership with Abijah, he secured financing for his factory and recruited a failed sailmaker from Scotland, John Brand, as his partner. Hunt managed the business affairs, such as purchasing and sales, and Brand was the production manager.[133]

In 1803, the pair shipped their first hempen bagging materials for baling cotton to customers in the Deep South. The opportunity was massive; each three-hundred-pound bale of cotton required approximately fifteen pounds of hempen baling materials. Cotton mills produced material by the ton. Hunt and Brand were wildly successful. Their success inspired others, and Lexington was quickly transformed into a hub of manufacturing activity filled with ropewalks and bagging factories. Hunt, an astute businessman, was aware of the laws of supply and demand and sold the hemp-bagging factory to Luke Usher and Company around 1813.[134]

The Kentucky hemp industry, which Hunt and Brand revolutionized, eventually transformed Lexington into what poet Josiah Espy described as "The Athens of the West":

> But Lexington will ever be,
> The loveliest and the best;
> A paradise thou'rt still to me,
> Sweet Athens of the West.[135]

Hunt sold his factory, but he continued in the hemp industry. He continued to grow hemp and act as a commission agent for hemp fiber and manufactured products. Hunt had spent the better part of his professional career building relationships. His buyers in Philadelphia and New Orleans knew that Hunt would not represent inferior product. Likewise, his friends in Kentucky who grew and manufactured hemp were confident that Hunt would get a fair price.[136]

Once Hunt amassed a significant fortune, he turned his attention to finance and public works. He was instrumental in bringing Transylvania University to Lexington in 1789 and in securing the land that allowed the university to move downtown. Hunt was also instrumental in the founding of the second psychiatric hospital in the nation, Eastern State Hospital, and served on its board of directors for twenty years.[137]

He and his wife, Catherine, raised eleven children. His oldest son, Charlton, was elected Lexington's first mayor after the city incorporated in 1832 and was responsible for starting Lexington's public school system.

Hopemont, the home of John Wesley Hunt, was built in 1814, shortly after Hunt sold his share of the bagging factory.

Charlton died of scarlet fever in 1836. Hunt's sons Abe and Thomas both eventually started hemp factories around the 1840s.[138] His daughter Henrietta married a merchant from Alabama, Calvin Morgan. Their son, John Hunt's grandson, John Hunt Morgan, rose to the rank of brigadier general in the Confederate army. John Wesley Hunt died during the cholera epidemic of 1849. He was seventy-six.[139]

John Wesley Hunt owned several properties in Lexington. His primary residence at 201 Mill Street, Hopemont, was completed in 1814. The historic home is now open to the public Wednesday through Sunday as a "living museum representing when Lexington was known as the 'Athens of the West' for its highly cultured lifestyle."[140] The home also features a small exhibit about Kentucky hemp history created in partnership with the Kentucky Hemp Heritage Alliance.

Henry Clay

Kentucky's most famous politician, Henry Clay (1777–1852), was actively engaged in the hemp industry on multiple levels throughout his career. Not only was Clay a hemp farmer, he also owned a stake in a spinning factory and promoted policies in Washington that helped the domestic hemp industry.

Clay was born in Hanover County, Virginia. His father, John Clay, died when Henry was just four years old. His mother, Elizabeth, married a man named Henry Watkins. When he was fifteen, Clay's mother and stepfather relocated to Versailles, Kentucky. Before they left, Watkins arranged for Henry to serve as deputy clerk in Virginia's High Court of Chancery.[141]

Clay's intelligence and work ethic attracted the attention of the chancellor, George Wythe, a scholar and law professor. Wythe, often credited with honing Clay's "mastery of the English language,"[142] employed Clay as his copyist and served as his mentor.

When he was ready, Clay took a position in the law office of former Virginia governor Robert Brooke in 1796. He earned his law license the following year and arranged to move to Kentucky. Henry settled in Lexington and quickly established himself as one of the best legal minds in the state. In 1799, he married Lucretia Hart, the daughter of prominent Lexington hemp merchant Thomas Hart.[143] Hart had moved to Lexington in 1794 with the expressed intent of opening a ropewalk.

In 1799, Clay campaigned in his first public election as a delegate to the Kentucky Second Constitutional Convention of 1799. In 1803, he was elected to the Kentucky legislature as a "Jeffersonian Republican." He served in the legislature until 1806, when he was appointed to fill the unexpired term of John Adair in the United States Senate. That started Clay's life of public service, which included terms in both houses of Congress and an appointment as secretary of state under President John Quincy Adams.[144]

One of Clay's most influential legacies was a series of protective tariffs and government-funded infrastructure projects collectively known as the "American System." This program was conceived as a way to encourage and protect domestic industries determined to be vital to the independence and growth of the new nation.[145] These protections extended to the hemp industry. Kentucky producers wanted their hemp used to outfit and rig the ships of the U.S. Navy. There was one major obstacle: geography. It was often cheaper for manufacturers on the Eastern Seaboard to import Russian hemp. Likewise, it was often cheaper for cotton producers to buy baling materials from Europe. The protections Clay advocated were mostly successful. During his political career, Kentucky evolved into an extremely wealthy and influential state, in large part because of the hemp industry.

Henry Clay's influence on Kentucky's hempstory is illustrated by the number of times and places his name appears in the narrative. Clay grew hemp at his Ashland estate in Lexington and was one of the principal shareholders of the Madison Hemp and Flax Company in Madison

Henry Clay's office, Mill Street, Lexington, Kentucky. Clay worked from this office from 1803 to 1810, when Mill Street was the center of hemp manufacturing.

County.[146] Clay's offhand comment about an impressive hemp stalk reportedly gave Hempridge, in Shelby County, its name. A note that one of Clay's sons sent to hemp merchant A.M. January & Sons in Maysville regarding a shipment of "coils of rope with my father's bagging"[147] indicates one of Clay's pet projects, the Lexington-Maysville Turnpike This may have been Kentucky's original "Hemp Highway."

Clay saw opportunity in the hemp industry and built his law office near Lexington's hemp manufacturing center. The office, which he occupied from 1803 to 1810, was within walking distance of the factories and homes of many of Lexington's leading hemp industrialists. This was concurrent with Clay's first term in the state legislature, his initial investment in the Madison Hemp and Flax Company and his first partial term as a U.S. senator.

The small (twenty feet by twenty-two feet) office structure is one of the few professional buildings remaining from this period of the city's history.[148]

Clay's home, Ashland, at 120 Sycamore Road, was completed around 1812 and is now a museum dedicated to Henry Clay's political and domestic life. A small educational hemp plot is grown on the grounds to facilitate discussion of Clay's involvement in Kentucky's hemp industry.

JOHN HUNT MORGAN

The John Hunt Morgan marker is not specifically about hemp; rather, it references hemp manufacturing as one of Morgan's "accomplishments."

> *John Hunt Morgan (1825–1864)—Leading cavalry raids behind enemy lines, General J.H. Morgan disrupted Union supplies and communications. For southerners, he was the ideal romantic hero. Captured in Indiana-Ohio raid, he escaped and was killed in Greeneville, Tennessee, September 4, 1864. Buried in Lexington Cemetery. Morgan became a courageous symbol of the Lost Cause. (over)*
>
> > *Known as the "Thunderbolt of the Confederacy," Morgan was born in Huntsville, Alabama; in 1831 moved to Lexington. After attending Transylvania, he fought in the Mexican War. In Lexington, he prospered as owner of hemp factory and woolen mill. Morgan organized the Lexington Rifles Infantry, 1857; later led them to aid Confederacy.*[149]
> >
> > —*Marker 1809, currently being relocated*

While hemp is only a portion of this marker's narrative, its inclusion offers an opportunity to explore the myth of the "Lost Cause," Morgan's true legacy and Kentucky's role in the rebellion. The facts suggest that far from the "ideal romantic hero" and courageous symbol of the Lost Cause, Morgan was actually vain, insubordinate rogue whose primary cause was preservation of his privileged life as an owner of enslaved people.

John Hunt Morgan was born into a family that first arrived in America in 1636, when James Morgan emigrated from England and settled in Connecticut. Morgan family lore was filled with pioneering men with a history of military service. John's great-grandfather Gideon Morgan (1751–1830) served as a corporal in the Connecticut Regiment during the Revolutionary War. His great-uncle Gideon Jr. served under General Andrew Jackson during the War of 1812. Jackson appointed Morgan command of a regiment of four hundred Cherokee warriors. During the 1813 campaign against the Creek Indians of the Mississippi Territory, Gideon Morgan Jr.'s unit attacked the Creek village of Hillabee in an atrocity known as the "Hillabee Massacre."[150]

Luther Morgan (born July 4, 1776), John's grandfather, was a skilled woodsman and pioneer merchant who followed the frontier to Alabama, where he settled near Huntsville. Luther Morgan often sent his twin sons, Calvin and Alexander, to Lexington, Kentucky, to contract for hempen baling materials. On one of these trips, Calvin Morgan met and began courting Henrietta Hunt, daughter of Lexington millionaire John Wesley Hunt. Calvin was different from other men in the Morgan family. He was far more reserved and discrete than his father, uncles and brothers. Calvin's serious and thoughtful nature passed muster with John Wesley Hunt, who blessed the marriage.[151]

Calvin and Henrietta married on September 24, 1823, and set up house in Huntsville, where Calvin opened an apothecary shop and served as an agent for his father-in-law. However, in 1831, Calvin Morgan, Henrietta and their four children (John, five; Calvin Jr., three; and two baby sisters, Catherine and Ann) were forced to move to Lexington during a bust cycle in the cotton industry. John Wesley Hunt hired Calvin to manage one of his farms, and the Morgan family lived in his farmhouse, Shadeland, on Tates Creek Road.[152]

John Hunt Morgan was schooled at home until the age of seventeen.[153] Raised in wealth and comfort, he was a scion of southern aristocracy. His father, Calvin, hoped that John and his younger brother Calvin Jr. would take full advantage of this privilege, especially the opportunity to get a world-class education. He wrote to his sons about the joy of getting a formal education while on business in Europe. "What a pleasure it is to [be] well informed. Without an education you can never be anybody. With it you may [be] the greatest in the land."[154]

The marker is correct. John attended Transylvania University, the school his grandfather John Wesley Hunt and a group of "public spirited citizens"[155] lobbied successfully to be moved from Danville to Lexington. Hunt also helped find Transylvania its first downtown home in modern-day Gratz Park. By the time John Hunt Morgan enrolled, Transylvania was highly regarded.

John was never interested in becoming educated, however, and his academic career was highlighted by drunken shenanigans, not academic accolades. John may have joined the prestigious Adelphi Society, but his motivation was their reputation for drinking. John also developed a reputation for spending time on the university's main lawn, where he liked to "swear at passersby."[156]

John's academic career ended in predictably flamboyant fashion. He and another member of the Adelphi Society, Richard Blanchard, took their debate to the next level when John challenged Blanchard to a duel. While no one was injured, dueling was and remains illegal in Kentucky. On July 4, 1844, both students were suspended by the university for one year.[157] This

Shadeland, the house on John Wesley Hunt's farm on Tates Creek Road, where his grandson John Hunt Morgan was raised.

must have deeply disappointed his grandfather, John Wesley Hunt, whose home was across the street from the university.

Raised on tales of the Morgan family's military adventures and frontier exploits, John Hunt Morgan yearned to write his own chapter in the family service record. Following his suspension from Transylvania, he applied for but did not receive a commission in the U.S. Marine Corps.[158]

The Mexican-American War (1846–48) finally provided John Hunt Morgan the opportunity for military glory he desperately sought. At the onset of the war, Morgan volunteered and was commissioned as a lieutenant under the command of General Zachary Taylor.[159] His unit participated in the Battle of Buena Vista, where, matched against an army of regulars commanded by Mexican general Santa Anna, the Kentucky volunteers distinguished themselves. Following a year of service, in 1847, the volunteers returned to Lexington to a hero's welcome.[160]

After the war, Morgan turned his attention to business. His first venture was a partnership with his friend Sanders Bruce. They purchased several enslaved people, whom they hired out as contract labor for such tasks as "hauling hemp, lumber, corn and other items." The business was profitable, and they reinvested their profits in more enslaved people.[161]

In 1848, John married Rebecca Bruce, Sanders's sister. The marriage united two of the biggest and most successful names in the hemp industry. After the wedding, the couple moved in with Rebecca's widowed mother,

Margaret. The Bruce home was located directly across the street from his grandfather's home, Hopemont.[162]

John Wesley Hunt died of cholera in 1849. He left his Hopemont home and a significant inheritance to his daughter Henrietta Morgan, John Hunt Morgan's mother. In 1853, Henrietta helped John and his brother Calvin Jr. open a manufactory for hempen goods.[163] Like his grandfather, John did well in the hemp industry. In the 1850s, competition in the hemp industry was fierce. Many businesses failed.[164]

John also mimicked his grandfather's success in the interstate traffic in enslaved people, with one significant difference. His grandfather supplied labor to cotton and sugar plantations in the Deep South. Morgan's model was more nefarious. He partnered with a human trafficker named Lewis Robards. Robards, the "most notorious dealer in Lexington," specialized in "young mulatto girls suitable for sale as mistresses or 'fancy girls' in New Orleans."[165]

While Morgan was successful in business, his personal life was dramatic. During pregnancy, his wife, Rebecca, developed "septic thrombophlebitis," an infected blood clot in her leg that rendered her an invalid for the rest of her life. The tragedy was compounded by the stillbirth of their child. Following the tragedy, Rebecca became depressed and withdrawn; John responded by immersing himself in the pleasures of antebellum aristocracy, of "virtuous manhood that permitted swearing, gambling, drinking and wenching."[166]

As the 1850s closed, Morgan was at peace.

> *He had found balance and harmony in the Southern system of honor. His invalid wife was dependent on him and in no position to question his manhood or challenge his headship of the family....He thoroughly identified with the Southern way of life; his self-esteem, his emotional equilibrium, his very identity depended on it. When Southern civilization was threatened, Morgan's own adjustment was threatened.[167]*

Morgan never abandoned his dreams of military heroics. Prior to the Civil War, Morgan organized a militia unit, the Lexington Rifles. In 1859, Kentucky elected pro-South Democrat Beriah Magoffin as governor. Magoffin and the state legislature commissioned a "state guard" in 1860. Three "units" volunteered for this service. Morgan's Lexington Rifles sympathized with secessionists. The two other units, the Old Infantry and the Lexington Chasseurs, supported the Union. Morgan's brother-in-law, business partner and friend Sanders Bruce joined the Lexington Chasseurs.[168]

At the outbreak of the Civil War, Morgan delayed volunteering to remain at the side of his ailing wife, Rebecca. However, he raised the Confederate flag over his factory and switched to exclusively manufacturing gray uniforms. After a ban on trade with secessionist states was enacted, Morgan attempted to run the blockade with two wagonloads of Confederate gray "Morgan jeans."[169]

Rebecca died on July 21, 1861, the same day as the First Battle of Bull Run.[170] After her death, Morgan planned for the Lexington Rifles to join the Confederate force in western Tennessee. On September 20, 1861, Morgan and around two hundred men raided the warehouse, where state-issued rifles for the militia were stored. They seized the rifles and escaped into the Southern lines.[171]

Morgan arrived at the Confederate camp on October 1 and was sworn into service on October 27, 1861. Between arriving at camp and Morgan's official entry into service, he led raiding parties behind Union lines, capturing food and military supplies and gathering intelligence. His disregard for military protocol should have raised concerns, but his initiative earned Morgan the command of a cavalry unit and the freedom of action he coveted.[172]

Morgan's initial actions were small raids behind enemy lines that created confusion and disrupted Union supplies. His reputation was enhanced by what his superiors considered brilliant rearguard action during the Confederate retreat from Nashville following the surrender of Fort Donelson in February 1862.

Toward the end of March 1862, Morgan decided he deserved leave. Without the permission or knowledge of his superiors, he departed for Richmond, Virginia, to pursue bourbon, poker and prostitutes. While Morgan was en route to Richmond, orders arrived at his command post ordering the Raiders to join the Confederate force mobilizing to retake Nashville. Morgan's second-in-command, Lieutenant Basal Duke, received the orders and immediately telegrammed Richmond, summoning Morgan's return. While Morgan caught the first train back to the front, Duke marched the Raiders toward their rally point.[173]

The Battle of Shiloh (April 6–7, 1862) was the most significant engagement in which the unit participated. Luckily for Duke, the unit was held in reserve. It saw its only action of the battle after Morgan resumed command, and a "single calvary charge was the contribution of Morgan's command to the Battle of Shiloh."[174] Following the Confederate defeat, Morgan was again asked to provide rearguard action to cover the retreat of the Confederate army. Again, Morgan excelled, earning the praise of his superiors.

After Shiloh, Morgan and the Raiders undertook their most successful operations of the war. During this period, Morgan established his reputation as the "Thunderbolt of the Confederacy."

Morgan's first raid into Kentucky (July 4–28, 1862) provided the foundation for the Morgan legend. During the raid, Morgan had George "Lightning" Ellsworth, a telegraph operator, listen to Union transmissions to gather intelligence. Morgan also used Ellsworth to transmit disinformation about the Raiders' location, movements and strength. Morgan's novel use of the telegraph earned the attention of the *London Times*, which declared, "Ellsworth's intelligence gathering the first and most striking innovation in the war."[175]

Morgan also used Ellsworth to communicate directly with sympathetic newspapers, feeding them stories that helped create the Morgan legend.

Morgan's most significant strategic action was the "Gallatin Raid" of August 12, 1862. Gallatin, Tennessee, was located near tunnels for the Louisville and Nashville Railroad, a vital supply line for the Union's advance on Chattanooga. After defeating the Union garrison, Morgan's men destroyed the tunnels. The damage closed the railroad for ninety days and forced Union general Don Carlos Buell to abandon his advance on Chattanooga.[176]

Emboldened by these successes, Morgan lobbied his superiors to invade Kentucky, claiming that "20,000–30,000 Kentuckians were anxious to join the Confederate Army."[177] Based on Morgan's "intelligence," the Confederates developed a plan that revolved around an invasion force of 16,000 troops supported by a wagon train loaded with 20,000 rifles for the new recruits. But the recruits Morgan promised never materialized. The invasion came to a head and the Confederates repulsed at the Battle of Perryville on October 8, 1862.

Outraged at their defeat, Morgan fell out of favor with his superiors. General Braxton Bragg attempted to reassign the Raiders. But Morgan's second-in-command, Basal Duke, never relayed those orders to Morgan. Bragg, with bigger problems with which to contend, did not follow up on the transfer.

In the summer of 1863, Morgan believed only a successful raid into Union territory would help him regain favor. He requested permission and supplies from his superiors, who denied his request. Morgan seemingly revised his plan and asked for permission to attack the Union garrison of 300 men stationed in Louisville. General Bragg, already snakebit from Morgan's previous actions, reluctantly approved the raid. By the time his force entered Kentucky, Morgan had 2,400 men under his command.

The "Great Raid" (July 1–26, 1863) was conducted concurrently with the end of the Siege of Vicksburg (May 18–July 4) and the Battle of Gettysburg (July 1–3). Had Morgan followed his orders and engaged General Ambrose Burnside's garrison in Louisville, his force of 2,400 men could have temporarily occupied the city. They could have destroyed the ports and rail hubs and threatened Union supply lines downriver. The threat would have required immediate attention. Finally, had Morgan actually occupied Kentucky's largest city, it may have helped recruit more Kentuckians to the Confederacy.

But Morgan was apparently more interested in headlines than strategy. He disobeyed orders and crossed the Ohio River into Indiana before ever reaching Louisville. Once in Union territory, his force led Union troops on a chase through Indiana and into Ohio. But Morgan had no exit plan. He, along with most of his command, were captured in northeast Ohio, just south of Youngstown. That November, Morgan escaped, further enhancing his legend. From a publicity perspective, the raid and Morgan's subsequent escape were successful; militarily, the raid was a disaster that resulted in the capture of most of Morgan's command. Had Morgan followed his orders and attacked Louisville, it would have presented a tangible strategic threat that Union forces could not have ignored.

While Morgan's repeated insubordination certainly warranted disciplinary action or even court-martial, the reality was that the Confederacy need experienced officers, and Morgan was a folk hero in the Southern press. To the public, Morgan was the leader of the "Great Raid" who escaped capture by the Yankees. He was not an insubordinate officer.

Morgan was assigned command of a regiment in southwest Virginia with the intent to provide support to General William "Grumble" Jones's attempt to repel the Union advance down the Shenandoah Valley. But Morgan had other plans. No sooner had he reported to his new assignment than he started to plan his next raid. Morgan even raised the morale of his poorly supplied soldiers by reading them a list of supplies they were sure to find behind Union lines.[178]

Morgan did not ask his superiors for permission to undertake the raid until after his troops had already started marching. General Bragg and the senior staff essentially threw up their hands in frustration.[179] Morgan's troops entered Kentucky on June 1, 1864. Unlike his first Kentucky raid, Morgan's troops did not conduct themselves honorably and were accused of a slew of "depredations," including the looting and pillaging of private property. Morgan was soundly defeated at the Battle of Cynthiana on June 11, 1864. He and his men had limited ammunition and supplies. Once their ammunition was depleted, the entire command, including Morgan, dropped their weapons and fled.[180]

Morgan was killed in Greenville, Tennessee, on September 4, 1864. His command was surprised while bivouacked overnight. Morgan, cornered by Federal forces, was shot in the back while attempting to escape.[181]

After the war, the Morgan myth continued to grow. In the fall of 1867, John's mother, Henrietta Morgan, began the process of having her children disinterred and reburied in the Hunt family plot in Lexington Cemetery. Morgan's Lexington funeral on April 17, 1868, drew a large crowd of adoring public and news media. One reporter fawned, "Even now, an air of romance surrounds his forays." Another cast Morgan as a hero of the "Lost Cause," writing, "Whatever may be said about the right or wrong of the 'Lost Cause', no one could question the motives of those who carried the banner."[182]

The John Hunt Morgan statue was moved to the Confederate burial ground at Lexington Cemetery in 2017.

The term *Lost Cause* first came into use following General Robert E. Lee's surrender at Appomattox. The term attempted to frame the failed rebellion as a noble cause similar to the Scottish rebellion as expressed in the work of Sir Walter Scott. The term was an attempt to both justify and excuse the actions of those who participated in an armed rebellion against the government and to paint the antebellum South in romantic terms as a sort of paradise lost.[183]

The mythologizing of Morgan's Raiders was part of this larger reframing of the rebellion in sympathetic terms. Some of the myth was Morgan's own doing. The dispatches of his exploits that Morgan had transmitted to sympathetic newspapers in the South helped create the image of the "ideal romantic hero" mentioned in the marker. His brother-in-law and second-in-command, Basal Duke, also directly contributed to building the Morgan myth when he published *History of Morgan's Calvary* in 1867.

In 1906, during the ascendancy of Jim Crow laws across the South, the Kentucky chapter of the United Daughters of the Confederacy started a drive to have a statue of Morgan erected in Lexington. Matched by $7,500 provided by the state legislature, the statue was dedicated with great fanfare in October 1911.[184] It was erected on the grounds of the Fayette County Courthouse, near where enslaved people were auctioned in Lexington. The historical marker was erected near his statue sometime after 1949. Morgan's statue and that of another Confederate "hero" were relocated to the Lexington cemetery in 2017, following the Charlottesville, Virginia riot. The historical marker was also removed and as of this writing has not been relocated.

Transylvania University

Transylvania University was the first place of higher learning on the frontier. The name *Transylvania* literally means "on the other side of the woods." Chartered by the Virginia legislature in 1780, the school was originally set in Danville. Located near Kentucky's first permanent settlement, Transylvania first admitted students in 1785.

The school, situated on the outskirts of Danville, truly stood at the gates of the frontier. Between 1783, when land was first selected for the site, and 1790, seven of the thirteen trustees of the university were killed in Indian attacks.[185]

Meanwhile, by the late 1790s and early 1800s, Lexington had evolved into the economic and cultural hub of Kentucky. During this period, several of

"Old Morrison" was named for hemp industrialist and Transylvania University supporter Colonel James Morrison.

the town's leading citizens believed that Lexington was better suited as home for the school. In 1789, Transylvania was moved to Lexington, initially to the corner of Cooper Drive and Nicholasville Road (near where the UK football stadium now stands).[186]

In 1793, several prominent citizens formed the Transylvania Land Company for the purpose of purchasing land for a college campus. They selected "out lot no 6" from the original town plat, an area now occupied by Gratz Park. In 1794, classes commenced in a small brick building located where the Carnegie Center now stands. It was replaced in 1818 by a structure designed as a school building. Unfortunately, the original school building burned down in 1829. After the fire, the university erected a bigger building across Third Street named "Old Morrison," after the first chairman of the board of trustees, James Morrison.[187]

Early supporters of moving the university from Danville to Lexington included Nathaniel and Thomas Hart, Peyton Short, Thomas January and Charles Wilkins. Contributions from these wealthy hemp industrialists helped to keep the university solvent. Over time, the contributions of five trustees of the university helped to firmly establish and maintain Transylvania University as a centerpiece of higher learning in Lexington. These five trustees, referred to as the "5 Hempmen of the University"[188] by historian Charles Ambrose, are: James Morrison, John Wesley Hunt, Robert Stephen Todd, Henry Clay and Benjamin Gratz.

JAMES MORRISON

Born in 1755 in Cumberland County, Maryland,[189] Morrison served as a captain in the Revolutionary War,[190] where, in 1777, he saw action during the Battle of Saratoga. Morrison initially settled outside of Pittsburgh after the war, where he was elected the first sheriff of Allegheny County. But earlier, in 1774, Morrison had helped scout the Kentucky Territory with Colonel William Thomson. By 1792, Morrison had moved to Lexington, where he initially worked as a merchant.[191]

Morrison was one of the pioneers in establishing Lexington's hemp industry, first advertising to purchase "clean hemp" in the *Kentucky Gazette* in 1794.[192] Initially, Morrison took the hemp he purchased and transported it downriver for sale in New Orleans. Morrison later served as a quartermaster general during the War of 1812, using his position to promote Kentucky hemp products to the U.S. Navy.

Following the War of 1812, Morrison settled into a role as one of Lexington's most involved citizens. In 1819, he opened a hemp factory in partnership with recently arrived Benjamin Gratz and hemp hero of the Battle of Trafalgar, John Bruce. Morrison's experience working in the quartermaster's office during the War of 1812 and the connections he made during his tenure in this role, undoubtedly helped in the success of their enterprise. Each principal was equally important to their success, their skills diverse yet complementary. Morrison had sales contacts in the government, Gratz had the legal background and Bruce supplied the manufacturing expertise.

Morrison was also eager to leave an indelible mark on the town he helped develop, and he significantly contributed to the development of Transylvania University. Morrison, whose background did not include a formal education, served as the chairman of the board of trustees for Transylvania University from 1819 until his death in 1823.

In his will, Morrison left the university "$20,000 for a professorship at the college and willed the bulk of his estate, estimated at $50,000 to Transylvania."[193] While his estate took approximately six years to settle, and the final amount the university ultimately received is unknown, the pledge itself helped ensure construction of a new classroom building. "Old Morrison," built between 1830 and 1834, was designed by architect Gideon Shylock.

ROBERT SMITH TODD

Robert Smith Todd (1791–1849) was the son of Levi Todd, one of Lexington's original founders. Better known as Mary Todd Lincoln's father. Todd also generously supported the university, donating over 5,000 acres of land. Todd's family was already well established when he and his partner, Edward Oldham, purchased a hemp factory at "a bargain price" in 1819. Todd later acquired a 175-acre farm that produced a significant amount of hemp in the late 1840s.[194]

BENJAMIN GRATZ

Gratz Park is named for Benjamin Gratz (1792–1884), one of Lexington's most successful entrepreneurs during the hemp industry's golden era. His house at 231 North Mill Street was built in 1819.[195] Gratz purchased it in 1824 and renamed it Mount Hope.[196]

Benjamin Gratz's father, Michael, emigrated from Silesia, Prussia, to Philadelphia in 1759, joining his older brother Barnard, a merchant, fur trader and land speculator. The brothers had a supply depot in western Pennsylvania that serviced a territory that extended as far as the Mammoth Cave region of western Kentucky. They supported the revolution and entered into a couple of Revolutionary War contracts. One contract with the Virginia legislature was to supply Virginia's soldiers. The other contract, likely much more lucrative, was to supply the camps holding British and Hessian POWs. The brothers did extremely well and became civic leaders in Philadelphia, where they helped establish the city's first Jewish synagogue.

Born in Philadelphia, Benjamin Gratz graduated from the University of Pennsylvania in 1811. Before he continued with his studies, Benjamin enlisted in the Pennsylvania Volunteer troops in the War of 1812, where he attained the rank of second lieutenant. After the war, he studied law and was admitted to the bar in 1817.[197]

The Gratz family owned several tracts of land in Kentucky, and Benjamin moved to Lexington in 1819, initially practicing law.[198] Shortly after his arrival, Gratz entered into partnership with John Bruce and Colonel James Morrison to form one of Lexington's most extensive hemp factories. Morrison died in 1825, and Bruce died in 1834, leaving Gratz the sole surviving partner. He operated the factory until the onset of the Civil War.

Mount Hope, the home of Benjamin Gratz, for whom Gratz Park was named. He was the first Jewish settler in Lexington.

One of the larger establishments, operated by Gratz and Bruce in Lexington, included for the manufacture of bagging a "calender and Hemp House, capable of storing 60 tons of hemp." A hackling house 18 feet wide and 30 feet long; a "factory" 195 feet long 25 feet wide and two stories high, "calculated for 12 spinners each story;" and attached to the factory, a weaving house which contained spindles and looms. For making rope the company had a brick hemp house 40 feet long, 50 feet wide, and two stories high, capable of storing 200 tons of hemp, a brick spinning house 180 feet long and 32 feet wide, and a rope walk "extending 100 fathoms," or 600 feet.[199]

Gratz was engaged in several other projects that helped develop the city of Lexington. He was on the board of trustees for Transylvania University, helped established the Lexington Ohio Railroad in 1830 and helped establish Lexington's first public library.[200]

HOWARD GRATZ

Henry Howard Gratz (1824–1913), who went by Howard, was Benjamin's second son. Howard married Minerva Campbell Anderson, the daughter of Nicholasville hemp manufacturer Colonel Oliver Anderson. In 1850, Gratz and his father-in-law moved to Lexington, Missouri, where they opened a hemp factory. Anderson's manufacturing know-how and Gratz's business acumen was a successful pairing, and the two were initially very successful.

However, their partnership coincided with "Bleeding Kansas," a precursor to the Civil War that pitted proslavery Missourians against their abolitionist neighbors to the west. Anderson, who couched his fanatical support for slavery in the Old Testament, was actively engaged in the dispute. This made Gratz, whose sympathies lay with preserving the Union, uncomfortable. Gratz disbanded the partnership and returned to Lexington.

Gratz Park was the original home of Transylvania College. After a fire burned down the main hall, the college moved across Third Street when it was rebuilt. This left a greenspace between Mill and Market Streets called "College Lawn." The space served various functions over the years. It was a bivouac for Union troops during the Civil War and in the years after became an impromptu gathering spot. The resulting noise and commotion irritated Howard's father, Benjamin. In 1878, Howard Gratz reached an agreement with Transylvania University. He constructed a fence around the block and restricted access. Later, Howard claimed he had created "a resort for respectable white people. If it were a public park the visitors could not be restricted."[201]

JAMES WEIR HOUSE, AKA THE CARRICK HOUSE, 312 NORTH LIMESTONE

James Weir was one of Lexington's most successful hemp entrepreneurs. After moving to Lexington from North Ireland in 1788, he established an extensive ropewalk. Weir's factory specialized in manufacturing various types of line for maritime applications, including hand lead lines, deep-sea lines, log lines and housings.[202]

Weir was one of the few Kentucky hemp manufacturers who took advantage of the Napoleonic Wars to ship product to eastern markets.

The James Weir House was completed after his death. His hemp factory occupied the entire block bordered by Third and Limestone Streets, Lexington, Kentucky.

While shipping products directly east was still not practical, the inflated prices created by the Embargo Act and Non-Intercourse Act made shipping to Philadelphia via New Orleans profitable.[203] However, Weir, like many Kentucky producers, saw the War of 1812 as disruptive to business.[204]

The home, which Weir commissioned in 1832, was completed in the 1850s, after his death. It was at the heart of the thirty-acre industrial site that Weir owned. After his death, his descendants lived in the house. The ropewalk may have been operated by Bruce and Morgan prior to the Civil War.[205]

The Brand Home at Rose Hill, 461 North Limestone Street

John Stuart Brand (1775–1849) emigrated from Scotland, where he had been a sail cloth manufacturer. Brand was initially successful until the hemp embargo forced him to close his business. Pressed by his creditors, Brand and his wife fled to France, where a friend advised him of the opportunities in America. The Brands briefly stayed in Philadelphia before John learned that Kentucky was emerging as a center for hemp cultivation. The couple arrived in Lexington in the spring of 1802.[206]

His arrival in Lexington coincided with John Wesley Hunt's interest in hemp manufacturing. By late 1802, Hunt and Brand were partners in the first hemp bagging factory in the United States. Brand was the production manager, and his stake in the business was "a gift from his father in the form of machinery for manufacture of hemp."[207] They began shipping product in 1803 and partnered together for ten years.

In 1813, they dissolved the partnership and Brand set out on his own. Brand eventually owned the entire block bound by Fourth and Fifth Streets and Upper and Limestone Streets. His home, Rose Hill, occupies the corner bound by Fifth and Limestone Streets. His hemp factory was located behind the home.

Brand continued to be successful. In 1818, he returned to Scotland to square his "moral obligations" with his creditors. Furthermore, the shipload of tobacco that he had the sense to bring helped make the trip profitable. His return to pay his debts earned him significant recognition. One foreign journal called Brand the "one honest man in America."[208]

Hemp manufacturing was always subject to boom-bust cycles. When Brand went into business for himself, around 1813, there were eight bagging factories operating in Lexington. He observed that, in 1820, there were "not any in operation but my own."[209] And his motivation for keeping his factory open was "in order to give employment to the slaves."[210]

Brand, like many others who prospered in the hemp industry, got involved in many other projects. He was a major stockholder in the Lexington and Ohio Railroad, was on the committee to build the road from Lexington to Cincinnati and served as a councilman after the city was incorporated in 1832.[211]

In 1833, after Lexington's first cholera epidemic claimed the life of his son, Brand retired from hemp manufacturing. He died in 1849, during another outbreak of cholera. At his death, Brand's estate was valued at over $850,000. A simple shaft of brown granite from his birthplace in Montrose, Scotland, marks his grave site in Lexington Cemetery.[212]

The Heritage Hemp Trail Walking Tour of Gratz Park

The homes and older structures of downtown Lexington often display homages to the hemp industry.

The Kentucky Hemp Heritage Alliance has compiled a downtown walking tour centered on Lexington's Gratz Park and surrounding neighborhoods. Featuring several downtown homes linked to Lexington's hempstory, the tour provides a glimpse of how pervasive the industry was in Lexington and the amount of wealth it generated.

Walter Scott House, 416 West Third Street

Around 1845, Persicolas Scott operated a successful ropewalk on the block bound by Broadway, Second and Third Streets. After he retired, Pericolas left his hemp business to his sons Walter and James. James had run the business for his father toward the end of Pericolas's career, eventually taking over the company. Periscolas died in 1896. In 1897, James was struck with sudden paralysis, from which he died later that year. James's brother Walter Scott managed the business until he left

A "Green Man" in the masonry of the Walter Scott House, part of the Heritage Hemp Trail's Walking Tour of Gratz Park.

Lexington in 1903. The ornate house Walter built on Third Street stands as a testament to the wealth that hemp continued to generate after the Civil War.[213]

The business office of Peter and Thomas January's ropewalk, Third Street, Lexington.

Peter January Office, 322 West 3rd Street

One of Lexington's first settlers in 1795, Peter January operated a ropewalk on Mill Street between Second and Third Streets. This small brick building served as January's home and office. The ropewalk extended behind the office toward downtown.[214]

John Bruce

John Bruce was born in Northumberland, England, and learned the trade of rope making in London. In 1805, he lived in Gibraltar, where he met his wife, Margaret Ross Hutton, the daughter of a Scottish soldier on station. John helped set up and manage the hemp factories that supported the Royal Navy. The factories managed by Bruce provided sailcloth, the rope and rigging for Lord Horatio Nelson's fleet at the pivotal Battle of Trafalgar. Around 1810, John and Margaret immigrated to the United States, eventually settling in Lexington. Bruce, in partnership with Benjamin Gratz and James Morrison, opened one of the city's largest ropewalks.[215] The enterprise helped all three men become extremely wealthy.

Bruce apparently felt a great deal of gratitude and affection toward his business partners, as reflected in the names of his sons James Morrison Bruce and Benjamin Gratz Bruce and his daughter Rebecca Gratz Bruce Morgan.

William Wallace Bruce

William Bruce (1821–1896) was John Bruce's eldest son. Like his father, William operated a hemp manufactory in Lexington. William Wallace's hemp factory was located on "Lot no. 105" per the "initial town plat." The plot was bound by the "Maysville Turnpike" (North Limestone) on the southeast side and Seventh Street on the northwest. William acquired the land in 1844 from local builder John McMurtry, who had recently built a house on the site for the previous owner before acquiring the property for himself.

Following the Civil War, William Wallace subdivided some of the property to construct homes for his recently emancipated workers. The neighborhood, named "Brucetown," was bounded by Jenkins Alley, Dakota Street, Florida Street, Idaho Avenue and North Upper Street. Bruce even assigned the original house on the lot (his home) "residence number 1" and made it the "prize for a lottery" of homes for his employees.

The end of the Civil War and emancipation of former enslaved people created an advantageous opportunity for employers. In Kentucky, the greatest concentration of Black people was in the cities. This attracted more recently freed Black people who, because of postwar violence toward them, sought the safety offered in community. This created an abundance of cheap labor in Lexington. As a result, many Lexington hemp manufacturers continued

Former William Wallace Bruce hemp warehouse on North Limestone Street in Lexington, Kentucky.

to operate profitably, including William Wallace Bruce. He continued to operate the factory until his son-in-law William Loughridge took over shortly before the end of the nineteenth century.[216]

News of William Wallace's death was carried in several papers across the country. The *Chicago Tribune* ran his obituary notice on November 16, 1896. The *Tribune* wrote that Bruce died as "Lexington's wealthiest citizen" and noted that he had "made many improvements in hemp machinery and succeeded to his father's business as bagging manufacturer. In this he amassed his fortune."[217]

The three buildings still standing are "among the earliest surviving from this once major industry in Lexington." The buildings were constructed between 1855 and 1890. The oldest, located along Upper Street just south of the power plant, is "brick Warehouse number 3," which appears on the Sanborn map of 1890. Two other buildings are dated to earlier construction. They are now used as part of a car repair business.

James Lane Allen

James Allen (1849–1925) is one of Lexington's best-known novelists. The youngest of seven children, he graduated from the University of Kentucky in 1872. Allen wrote nineteen books, of which fourteen focused on or were set

Workers harvesting hemp in a hempfield near Lexington, Kentucky. Postcard printed by Art Mfg., Amelia, Ohio, 1909.

Fountain of Youth in Gratz Park, dedicated to the children of Lexington, by James Lane Allen.

in Kentucky, including *The Reign of Law: A Tale of the Kentucky Hemp Fields*. The novel, first published in 1900, uses Kentucky's hemp industry as a backdrop to explore controversial topics like "religious doubt and Darwinism."[218]

Allen, who spent his youth on a farm, Scarlet Gate, outside of antebellum Lexington, wrote in elegiac terms about the hemp fields of Kentucky. The descriptions he uses and his inherit understanding of activities on the hemp farm reveal a familiarity born from hours spent in the hemp fields of Lexington.

Allen describes life growing up at Scarlet Gate in the introduction to his novel *The Cardinal* (1894). While Allen laments the lack of contemporaries around him, he notes that this led him "to follow the negroes into the fields, where as one result I watched the hemp in all its changes."[219] Allen wrote that his experiences at Scarlet Gate instilled in him his love of nature and inspired his writing. "The question is often asked, how a man in the city can write of a country far away that he has not seen for years. But that country is never far away and the man looks over into it unceasingly. He has but to lift his eyes to see it—as clearly as he sees the people on the street.[220]

Scarlet Gate was acquired by the Lexington School, an adjacent private school, in 2011. The home now serves as the residence for the school's headmaster, while the twelve-and-a-half-acre lot provides students with a living laboratory in which to explore Kentucky wildlife.

In his will, Allen left money to the city. It was used to build the *Fountain of Youth* in Gratz Park in his honor. The fountain is located at the northern edge of the park, across the street from Morrison Hall.

6

FRANKLIN COUNTY HEMP

The hempstory told on Franklin County's historical markers represents one of Kentucky's longest historical narratives about hemp. Franklin County has two of the fourteen roadside historical markers spanning the entire hemp narrative, from pioneer times until the end of hemp manufacturing in Kentucky in 1952. The markers are located within a mile of each other on US 421, Wilkinson Boulevard.

> *Franklin county was formed in the year 1794, and named in honor of the distinguished patriot and statesman, Dr. Benjamin Franklin. It lies on both sides of the Kentucky river….Hemp is cultivated to a limited extent.*
>
> *Frankfort is the seat of justice for Franklin county, and the capital of the state of Kentucky….It is beautifully situated on the Kentucky river… in the midst of the wild and romantic scenery which renders that stream so remarkable. Frankfort contains…three bagging factories.*[221]

Leestown

In 1773 McAfee Company and Hancock Taylor came here and surveyed area, an early pioneer stopping place. By 1775 Leestown settled and named by Hancock and Willis Lee; established by Va. Assembly, 1776. Temporarily abandoned in 1777 because of Indian attack, it was reestablished and became well-known shipping port for tobacco, hemp, corn and whiskey to New Orleans market.

Leestown: Va. General Assembly had tobacco inspection warehouse erected in Leestown, 1783. A hemp factory was here for many years. At one time Leestown was a commercial center and contender for the state capital. During War of 1812 it served as supply base against the Indians. In 1827 the stones for the Old State House were quarried from river bank near here.[222]

—*Marker 103, entrance to Buffalo Trace Distillery*

Leestown, the second settlement on the Kentucky River after Boonesborough, was named by its first settlers, Captain Hancock Lee and his brother Willis, in June 1775. After the settlement was temporarily abandoned in 1777,[223] it remained "abandoned for nearly ten years"[224] when the area was finally secured. Hancock Lee started selling lots to the public in 1789. He later offered Leestown as the state capital in 1792.

Nestled along the banks of the Kentucky River, the settlement evolved into an important industrial site and shipping point for sending goods downriver to markets in New Orleans. Early industrial activity included a warehouse and boatyard. Leestown served as an important supply hub and base of operations against the Indians and British during the War of 1812.

Several warehousing facilities were commissioned in Franklin County to inspect and store products securely before they were shipped downriver to market. "Stephen Arnold and William Payne were appointed…to locate and superintend the erection of a large store room for the reception of tobacco, flour and hemp."[225] A ferry was established at the ropewalks one mile above Frankfort, "across the Kentucky River from the lands of Elijah Craig, and an inspection of hemp and flour was established" in 1798.[226] Robert McKee was granted a license to build a warehouse to store tobacco, flour and hemp at the mouth of Benson Creek in 1811, while Richard Taylor was granted the right to build a hemp inspection warehouse at the mouth of Leestown Branch.[227]

In later years, Leestown was the home of Kentucky River Mills, before Leestown was officially annexed by the City of Frankfort.

Kentucky River Mills

Kentucky River Mills began making yarns for backs of Brussels carpets in 1878, and started producing binder twine in 1879. Finest quality imported machinery used. Employed 125 persons year-round. In 1941, received contract from Navy for $148,500 worth of marine oakum. This was the last hemp factory to operate in KY., closing down in 1952.[228]
—*Marker 1164, US 421, entrance to Jim's Seafood*

In the summer of 1878, a new hemp manufactory was incorporated in Frankfort: Kentucky River Mills. The original business plan called for the factory to "manufacture…yarns, twines, cloths and other fabric." The factory was in production by the end of 1878, "producing hemp yarn for Brussels carpets" with "hemp rope and twine…sideline products."[229] Kentucky River Mills quickly discovered "competing with eastern producers of carpet yarn was more difficult than foreseen."[230] In fact, Kentucky River Mills encountered the same obstacle that had historically stymied the Kentucky hemp industry. It was still cheaper for eastern manufacturers to import fiber and manufacture at their location than the landed cost of shipping Kentucky products across the country.

The history of the company might have been short if not for the invention of the reaper-binder in the late 1870s. A combination of two separate implements (the reaper and the binder), the reaper-binder was part of the industrialization of the farm that transformed agriculture and made large-scale farming feasible.

Prior to the reaper-binder, the grain harvest required a team of three people. One person drove the team of horses pulling the reaper, while another person stood on the reaper's metal apron, raking the grain into small piles called "gavels." The third person followed them, binding the small piles of grain with twine. William Deering & Company began mass-producing its reaper-binder in 1880, followed shortly to market by Cyrus McCormick. These two companies would later be part of the merger that created International Harvester.[231]

The invention sparked a huge demand for binder twine, and Kentucky River Mills was positioned perfectly to meet it. In 1880, the officers of Kentucky River Mills decided "to limit production to twine, string and rope." They specialized in binder twine.[232] Kentucky River Mills was one of several independent cordage and twine companies that operated in Kentucky, and the surging demand for binder twine temporarily revitalized

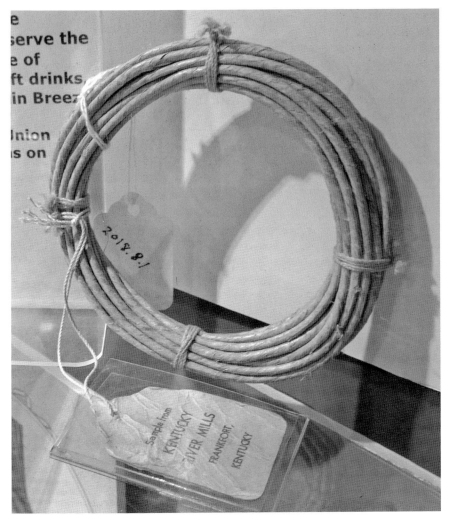

Hemp binder twine, like that Kentucky artist Paul Sawyier sold. From Kentucky River Mills, on display at the Capital City Museum, Frankfort, Kentucky.

the state's hemp industry. In the 1880s and 1890s, Kentucky once again led the nation in hemp production.

The company was fortunate to have started before the introduction of the reaper-binder. It allowed them to develop a network of customers and suppliers while there was still little competition. As competition increased, inconsistent quality and unreliable supplies of twine motivated equipment manufacturers to invest in their own captive twine mills.[233]

Paul Sawyier, Kentucky Artist

One of the principal investors in Kentucky River Mills was a local physician, Dr. Nathanial Sawyier. Outside of Sawyier having used his stock in the company as collateral for multiple personal loans, his investment in the mill would not be noteworthy. However, Nathanial Sawyier relaxed by dabbling in art, a hobby he was reported to have engaged in until his health no longer permitted, often sketching his family.[234] This passion for art was inherited by his son Paul (1865–1917).

In 1877, Nathanial's wife, Ellen, suggested they hire a private art teacher for their children. They hired Elizabeth Hutchins, a "mature maiden artist" from Cincinnati, to teach "outdoor sketching, china painting and flower painting" in the Sawyier home.[235] Paul, then twelve, showed an early aptitude for art. After completion of his general studies, Paul moved to Cincinnati to study portraiture. In 1889, he traveled to New York, where he studied at the New York Art Student League until early 1890.[236]

Perhaps to pay for his formal art studies, Paul worked as a traveling binder twine salesman. Business records, payroll stubs and correspondence indicate six distinct periods of employment between 1887 and 1893.[237] However, it appears that Paul was not enthusiastic about the job. Business correspondence preserved at the Kentucky Historical Society includes several letters imploring Paul to do a better of job of communicating while on the road.

Paul may not have enjoyed selling binder twine, but several of his paintings pay homage to the hemp industry, most notably *The Hemp Breaker* and *Breaking Hemp*.

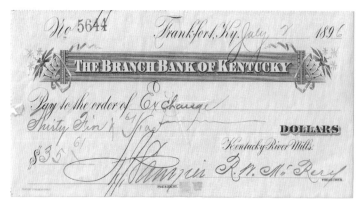

Kentucky River Mills check signed by Nathanial Sawyier, father of Kentucky artist Paul Sawyier. Isenstein private collection.

NEW OWNERSHIP

In 1937, Congress passed the Marihuana Tax Act of 1937. While it was not the intent of Congress, certain language in the law threatened the hemp industry. Yet, toward the end of 1938, Kentucky River Mills was invigorated by fresh investment from new ownership. Daniel Deronda "D.D." Stewart (1897–1974) was born in Knox County in southeastern Kentucky. He initially made his wealth in the coal industry before expanding into other industries, including hemp.

D.D. acquired controlling interest of Kentucky River Mills stock in 1938 and was elected company president. When he took over the company, Stewart stated that it was his goal to "revive hemp raising" in central Kentucky, which was "long lucrative in this section," and he "recalled the romantic stories built around the hemp raising industry…and the beauty of fields of hemp at various stages of growth."[238]

KENTUCKY RIVER MILLS AND THE USS *WASP*

The company not only manufactured cord, twine and rope but also manufactured a product called marine oakum. "Even the waste fiber from manufacturing processes (and old ropes which were picked apart when their strength was gone) became oakum, used in caulking the seams of wooden ships."[239]

Before the railroad opened new routes to market, most Kentucky exporters relied on rivers to bring products to market. From the early flatboats that transported goods downstream on the current, to the steamboats and paddle wheelers that made upstream river travel convenient, oakum was an essential shipbuilding material. Oakum is still used for caulking on ships and boats to help make them watertight and for repairing structural leaks in plumbing applications. For a navy stockpiling supplies in preparation for war, oakum was essential.

Kentucky River Mills supplied oakum to the navy even before it was awarded the contract for $148,500 in 1941. The previous year, the aircraft carrier USS *Wasp* (CV-7) was commissioned into the navy rigged with oakum from Kentucky River Mills. Up to 90 percent of the oakum used by the navy in the years prior to the war may have been supplied by Kentucky River Mills.[240]

Restricted in size by the Washington Naval Treaty, the *Wasp* was underpowered and lightly armored. When the United States entered World War II, the *Wasp* was assigned convoy protection and anti-submarine duty in the Atlantic Ocean. In early 1942, the *Wasp* played a key role in reinforcing the British Royal Air Force garrison at Malta. The *Wasp* was transferred to the Pacific theater after the Battle of Midway and was the only aircraft carrier to serve in both the Atlantic and Pacific theaters. In September 1942, the *Wasp* was sunk by Japanese Imperial Navy submarine *I-19* during the Battle for Guadalcanal.[241]

Jim's Seafood, 950 Wilkinson Boulevard, was built on the foundations of Kentucky River Mills. The restaurant features a small display about the mill in its waiting vestibule. The exhibit features historic pictures of the mill, copies of Sanborn insurance maps, hemp rope and some old hand tools used at the factory.

7

HEMP IN JEFFERSON COUNTY

Farmington

Jefferson County was one of the three original counties created when the Virginia legislature initially subdivided the Kentucky Territory in May 1780. Jefferson County is home to the state's largest city, Louisville, which was located, settled and developed specifically to help navigate the "Falls of the Ohio." The "falls," which drop approximately twenty-six feet over the course of two miles, was a significant obstacle to moving people and freight down the Ohio River and out to the Mississippi.[242]

> *Jefferson county was formed in 1780, by the Virginia legislature...and named in honor of Thomas Jefferson, distinguished, at that day, as the author of the declaration of independence, and one of the ablest and most efficient members of the continental Congress. This county is situated in the northwest middle part of the State—bounded on the north by Oldham and the Ohio river*
>
> *The face of the county is diversified, presenting, for miles around, and including the city of Louisville, an almost unbroken, level, plain, rich, productive and highly cultivated.*
>
> *The staples of Jefferson are hemp, wheat, corn, oats and potatoes.*
>
> *"The trade in Louisville is very extensive," and includes, "two steam bagging factories, producing about 2 million yards cotton bagging annually, 6 cordage and rope factories."*[243]

Hemp and slavery are inextricably entwined in Kentucky's early historical narrative. Jefferson County presents an opportunity to explore how the economics of the hemp industry influenced Kentucky's reliance on the labor of enslaved people. The historical marker "Farmington" in Jefferson County discusses an 1841 visit young Abraham Lincoln made to the family hemp plantation of his best friend, Joshua Speed. According to the marker, the visit helped clarify Lincoln's opposition to slavery. Crosstown Oxmoor Farm was the home of Alexander Scott Bullitt, an original pioneer and co-architect of Kentucky's first state constitution. Bullitt and his descendants were involved in helping to draft all three of the state's antebellum constitutions. The Bullitts also owned a hemp plantation and viewed enslaving people as essential to the industry.

WILLIAM CHRISTIAN

Colonel William Christian (1743–1786) showed an interest in the Kentucky territory long before he actually settled it. And his influence cannot be measured by the amount of time he lived here. Born in Staunton, Virginia, William Christian first volunteered for military service when he was fifteen, serving as a captain in the Second Virginia Regiment during the French and Indian War.[244]

Following the war, he worked and studied law under Patrick Henry. While under Henry's employ, William Christian met and married Patrick's sister, Anne. Christian continued military service. By 1774, he had ascended to the rank of lieutenant colonel in the Second Virginia Regiment and participated in actions against Indians along the Clinch River.[245] His unit was also dispatched to support Virginia governor Lord Dunmore at the Battle of Point Pleasant in October 1774, arriving after the Indians had been defeated.[246]

In 1775, at the onset of the American Revolution, Christian was commissioned as a lieutenant colonel in the First Virginia Regiment, commanded by his brother-in-law Colonel Patrick Henry. Henry, however, accepted a commission with the regular Continental army, and command of the First Virginia was offered to William Christian.

Christian resigned this commission after a month to lead an independent expedition of 1,200 men against nearby Over Hill Cherokee. He soon sent a report to the Virginia House of Delegates that he had returned from his expedition, treaty in hand that ceded large tracts of Tennessee and Kentucky to Virginia.[247]

William Christian cabin at the Oxmoor estate, Louisville, Kentucky. Christian, an early advocate for statehood, is buried in the small family cemetery nearby.

When he returned, William Christian joined the militia, where he focused on suppressing any Tory activity. In 1781, General Nathanial Greene appointed Christian head of a commission empowered to negotiate a treaty with the Cherokee in the western territories. After the settlers were defeated at the Battle of Blue Licks, Christian suggested he be given a command of one thousand men to protect the settlements. In 1782, he also suggested the construction of a gunboat to patrol the Ohio River. Christian's service in the French and Indian War was compensated with a land grant along Beargrass Creek.[248] But legislative and other duties prevented him from leaving Virginia for several years.

When William Christian finally settled in Kentucky in May 1785, his homestead was located next to the farm started a year earlier by Alexander Scott Bullitt. Bullitt was the son of a prominent Virginia judge and, like Christian, was an advocate for Kentucky statehood. That fall, Christian's oldest daughter, Priscilla, married Alexander Bullitt.

Indian attacks continued after the war. In the spring of 1786, a small raiding party ransacked Sturgus's station near the Christian and Bullitt homesteads. William Christian and Alexander Bullitt led a group of settlers that pursued the raiding party back across the Ohio River, trapping two of the raiding Indians. In the ensuing skirmish, William Christian was shot and mortally wounded.[249]

Christian County was named in his honor in 1796.[250]

Oxmoor Farm

Alexander Scott Bullitt (1762–1816) was born in Dumfries, Virginia. His father, Cuthbert, an attorney and judge on the Virginia Court of Appeals, planned for his son to follow in his footsteps. Alexander showed an aptitude for politics, serving as a member of the Virginia House of Delegates in 1782.

In 1783, as part of a militia assignment, Bullitt migrated to Kentucky. He initially settled near Bull Skin Creek in current Shelby County. However, isolated and vulnerable to Indian attacks, he relocated east of Louisville and established a hemp plantation, Oxmoor Farm, in 1786.

Alexander Bullitt and his wife, Priscilla, inherited property from her father's estate, enlarging Oxmoor. Alexander was a successful hemp farmer and actively engaged in politics. Like William Christian, Alexander was a vocal advocate for Kentucky statehood.

Alexander was a delegate at Kentucky's first Constitutional Convention in Danville in 1792, where he and George Nichols drafted the first state constitution. After Kentucky was admitted into the Union, Bullitt was elected one of the eleven original state senators. His peers elected him Speaker of the Senate, a position he held until 1800.

The state held a second constitutional convention in 1799, in part to address the issue of executive succession. Once again, Bullitt was a delegate and one of the architects of the new constitution. The succession question was addressed by creating the office of lieutenant governor, a position to which Bullitt was elected in 1800. He was elected to a term in the senate in 1804 before he retired from public life in 1808.

Alexander and Priscilla Bullitt had four children, two boys and two girls. Priscilla died in November 1806, perhaps influencing Alexander's withdrawal from public service. He remarried, to Mary Prather in July 1807, and fathered three more children before his death in 1816. He is buried in the family plot at the Oxmoor estate.[251]

William Christian Bullitt

William Christian Bullitt (1793–1877) grew up at Oxmoor and took over the family farm after his father passed. He inherited his father's love of hemp farming but not his political aspirations. William Christian Bullitt served in an elected capacity once, as a reluctant if not vocal delegate at Kentucky's third constitutional convention in 1849.

Several of the issues being debated during the convention were related to slavery. Lead by Cassius Marcellus Clay, abolitionists forced a debate on ending slavery. However, they were squarely in the minority, as most of the delegates agreed with Bullitt, the reluctant delegate, whose impassioned speech carried the day:

> *The free states do not, and will not raise hemp and tobacco. Kentucky and Missouri have the monopoly of this great article, hemp. This, as long as slavery remains, must be the case.…Take away slaves, and you destroy production of that valuable article, which is bound to make the rich lands of Kentucky and Missouri still more valuable.*[252]

Kentucky's third constitution not only reaffirmed the legality of slavery but also strengthened the rights of slave owners and bounty hunters seeking enslaved people who had escaped. After the new state constitution was ratified, William Christian Bullitt retired from politics and returned to his hemp plantation.

The economic advantage created by slavery is irrefutable. The labor of enslaved people directly increased profits and generated more wealth for industrialists. This fact was reaffirmed in 1838, when David Myerle opened Louisville's first steam-powered ropewalk. The facility was 1,100 feet long and 25 feet wide, with the latest rope-twisting machinery running the length of the building. Myerle utilized both Whites and enslaved Black people in his factory. Myerle stated that he found, "the cost of manufacturing cordage was one-third less with slave labor."[253]

Farmington

Historic residence completed in 1816 for John and Lucy (Fry) Speed. The Jefferson Inspired plan by Paul Skidmore includes octagonal rooms, rare in 19ᵗʰ c. Kentucky. As many as 62 African-Americans enslaved at

Farmington plantation of James Speed. An 1841 visit by Abraham Lincoln helped cement Lincoln's opposition to slavery.

Farmington worked the 550-acre hemp plantation. Abraham Lincoln spent 3 weeks here in 1841 as guest of the family of his closest friend, Joshua Speed.

After his visit, Lincoln described a group of shackled slaves he saw on his steamboat trip home. Later he called the memory a "continual torment to me." During Civil War the Speeds supported the Union and Joshua's ties to Lincoln helped secure Kentucky for the Union. Lincoln appointed James Speed Attorney General in 1864.[254]

—Marker 2231, 3033 Bardstown Road, Louisville

Captain James Speed (1739–1811), born in Mecklenberg County, Virginia, served in the Continental army during the Revolutionary War. He was wounded at the Battle of Guilford Courthouse on March 15, 1781. The wounds ended his military career and, like many, he was offered land grants in the Kentucky Territory as part of his compensation. Speed and his family migrated to Kentucky over the Wilderness Road in 1782 and settled in Danville.[255]

James's son John Speed (1772–1840) moved to Jefferson County with his second wife, Lucy Fry Speed, in 1810. He had purchased five hundred acres along Beargrass Creek and established a hemp plantation he called Farmington.

Their son Joshua Fry Speed (1814–1882) left Kentucky in 1835 and moved to Springfield, Illinois, where he worked merchandising and helping edit a local newspaper.[256] There he met Abraham Lincoln, who had recently been admitted to the Illinois bar. Speed offered Lincoln a place to stay, and the two became best friends.

Lincoln's visit to the Speed family plantation was a profoundly life-changing event. In 1841, Lincoln stayed at the Speed plantation for three weeks. The visit was significant in at least two ways. Lincoln made an excellent impression on the Speeds, building a connection that helped him politically in the future. During his stay, Lincoln experienced prolonged exposure to slavery. This included a "tormenting" encounter on the steamboat trip back home.

Between 1790 and 1860, over one million enslaved people were transported to the Deep South in support of the cotton industry. As Kentucky's antebellum economy evolved, one of the evil "industries" that emerged was the interstate traffic in enslaved people. While tobacco and especially hemp farming were dependent on the labor of enslaved people, in strictly economic terms Kentucky had an oversupply of enslaved persons. In 1801, John Wesley Hunt helped create Kentucky's interstate slave trade, which expanded rapidly once the federal government banned the transatlantic trafficking of enslaved people in 1808. By the 1840s, Louisville was one of the largest markets for enslaved people in the country.

The work on the cotton and sugar plantations of the Deep South was extremely harsh and demanding. As a result, enslaved males were in higher demand. One of the most devastating practices of slavery was breaking apart families. The interstate traffic in enslaved people exacerbated this vile practice, which came to be known as getting "sold down the river." Harriet Beecher Stowe captured the pain this practice had on the families of enslaved people in her classic novel *Uncle Tom's Cabin*.[257]

The election of 1860 was extremely contentious. There were four candidates seeking office, including Lincoln's main rival, Democrat Stephen Douglas. The vice president, Democrat John C. Breckinridge of Kentucky, and Constitutional Union Party nominee John Bell were on the ballot. The Republican Party's antislavery platform meant Lincoln was not even on the ballot in ten Southern states. However, the proslavery vote was split. Vice President Breckinridge came in second, winning the nine states of the Deep South but failing to win his home state. Breckinridge was followed by Bell, with Douglas coming in last.[258]

Seven Southern states had already seceded from Union by the time Lincoln was inaugurated on March 4, 1861. Four more states left the Union shortly afterward. South Carolina was the outspoken leader of the secessionist movement. On April 12, 1861, South Carolina militia attacked and seized control of Fort Sumter from Federal troops, starting the American Civil War.[259]

At the outbreak of hostilities, the Confederacy lobbied Kentucky to join the cause, and there was strong reason to believe Kentucky's sentiments lay with the South. The president of the Confederacy, Jefferson Davis, was a Kentucky native. Outgoing vice president and presidential candidate John C. Breckinridge, a Lexington native, organized a provisional Confederate government in Kentucky and accepted a commission in the Confederate army.

Southern war planners also recognized the military advantage of having the Ohio River as their northern border. Confederate leaders wanted to limit fighting in the Deep South to preserve their economies. If Kentucky joined the cause, it would have created a defensible border and shifted frontlines significantly north. However, due in large part to Lincoln's relationship with the Speeds and their influence in the commonwealth, Kentucky remained in the Union. Lincoln appointed James Speed his attorney general and offered the position of secretary of the treasury to his friend Joshua. However, Joshua refused, preferring to remain Lincoln's special advisor on "Western Affairs."[260]

SISTERS ON OPPOSING SIDES

The Civil War not only divided the nation; it also literally divided families. Family histories in Kentucky and other border states are filled with stories of brothers joining opposing armies. Louisville's story exposes the other side of the conflict, sister against sister.

John and Lucy Fry Speed lived on a hemp plantation that enslaved at least sixty-two people. However, their sons James and Joshua were both abolitionists. And the family supported Lincoln and preserving the Union. Across town, another hemp farmer, William Christian Bullitt, was one of Kentucky's most outspoken supporters of slavery. His wife, Mildred Fry Bullitt, was Lucy Fry Speed's younger sister.

LOUISVILLE HEMP AFTER THE CIVIL WAR

As with most areas in Kentucky, Louisville's hempstory continued after the Civil War. After the war, urban centers like Louisville and Lexington saw an influx of freed Blacks from rural areas. The resulting competition for jobs kept wages low. The end of slavery also helped accelerate the adoption of automation in manufacturing. Hemp bagging, cordage and baling materials were still necessary agricultural commodities. Factories like the Louisville Bagging Company were ideally located to meet these needs.

8

JESSAMINE COUNTY HEMP

One of chief producing counties, it was third in value of product and also in number of cordage factories, with 14 in 1840. Peak production reached in the late 1800s, yielding over 1,000 tons per year; with a value of $125,000. In 1899, it was one of the three Bluegrass counties which together produced more than one-half of hemp grown in the entire country.[261]
—Marker 1315, Jessamine County Courthouse, Nicholasville

Jessamine County was formed out of Fayette County in 1798. The county seat of Nicholasville was named after local resident George Nichols, who, along with Alexander Scott Bullitt, helped draft Kentucky's first state constitution in 1792. Hemp was an established crop by 1796, and by 1840, Jessamine County was responsible for two-thirds of the state's hemp production. In 1870, the county was still producing 1.8 million pounds annually.[262]

That portion of Jessamine which is comprised within the boundary appropriately termed "the garden of Kentucky," presents a slightly undulating surface, and black, friable, and remarkably rich soil-producing luxuriant crops of hemp, corn and grass. Hemp is the staple.

Nicholasville, the county seat...contains 4 bagging factories. Situated in the heart of a fine country, and surrounded by a rich and intelligent population, Nicholasville is necessarily a place of considerable business.[263]

Hemp manufacturing quickly developed into a significant portion of Nicholasville's economy: "Manufacturers of bagging were George I. Brown, Moreau Brown, George Brown, Henry Metcalf, William Scott and Colonel Oliver Anderson."[264]

George I. Brown

George I. Brown (1784–1856) was born in North Carolina and moved to Franklin County, Kentucky, with his parents in 1791. He moved to Nicholasville in 1811 and initially operated a dry goods store on Main Street.[265]

Around 1817, Brown bought some property south of Nicholasville and began farming and manufacturing hemp. George Brown was "probably the pioneer of hemp manufacture in Jessamine."[266] He was also very active in politics and was elected to several terms in both houses of the Kentucky legislature.

In the early 1850s, he began construction of his "brick Gothic cottage," Edgewood, near downtown Nicholasville. Brown died in 1856, not long after the home was completed. The house remains a private residence and now anchors a residential neighborhood in Nicholasville. It is relatively unchanged from the original design.[267]

George I. Brown home, Nicholasville, Kentucky, built in the early 1850s. Brown died in 1856, not long after it was completed.

George Brown

George Brown (1819–1897) was born in Nicholasville. After he completed his schooling, which included studying at both Centre College in Danville and Transylvania University in Lexington, George started a hemp factory. He had learned hemp manufacturing from his father, who helped pioneer the industry in Lexington.[268]

In 1843, he married the appropriately named Anne M. Hemphill (1826–1888), described as "an affectionate, faithful and helpful wife… one of the model housekeepers of Jessamine County." After her death, George purchased one of the most ornate headstones in the Maple Grove Cemetery.[269]

In 1853, Brown moved his family to a home he had constructed on his farm along Jessamine Creek. The farm was also the base for his hemp-manufacturing business.[270]

Captain Oliver Anderson

Oliver Anderson (1784–1873) was born in Nicholasville. Industrious at an early age, one of the first businesses Oliver started was floating goods downriver on flatboats to markets in New Orleans. He then walked back to Kentucky over the Natchez Trace to begin the process anew. Anderson served in the War of 1812, rising to the rank of lieutenant. He stayed in the military after the war, attaining the rank of lieutenant colonel before resigning in 1820.[271]

He returned to central Kentucky and, by 1830, had entered into the hemp industry as both a hemp producer and a manufacturer of rope and bagging. Anderson initially partnered with Samuel G. Jackson, a textile producer, to form the Anderson & Jackson Company. The firm did well for many years before a decrease in demand for Kentucky hempen goods forced it into dissolution.[272]

Anderson remained engaged in the Kentucky hemp industry until around 1850. He then decided to relocate his family from Kentucky to Lexington, Missouri. This included his son-in-law Howard Gratz, whose own family was very successful in the hemp industry in Lexington, Kentucky. The younger Gratz was a sharp businessman, and they were very successful in Missouri. Howard Gratz was a partner in two businesses, one with Anderson and the other with Joseph O. Shelby, his stepbrother. Gratz and Shelby owned a ropewalk in Waverly, Missouri, while Anderson and Gratz's company was located in Lexington, Missouri. By 1854, Anderson and Gratz operated the largest manufacturing facility in the area.[273]

Anderson was a zealous advocate for slavery, stating: "Slavery is a scriptural institution, and…Abolitionists, as they exist here, are infidels. They are unwilling that God shall be judge of what is proper and right, and desire themselves to determine what is proper, and that too, in direct opposition to God's revealed law as given to the Hebrews. Hence, they say they want an Antislavery Bible and an Antislavery God."[274] By the mid-1850s, both Anderson and Shelby were deeply involved in the "Bleeding Kansas" campaign, the growing border war between Missouri and Kansas. The rhetoric and violence unnerved Gratz, who sold his share of Anderson and Gratz and returned to Kentucky in 1856. Anderson floundered on his own and probably would have been lost to history had it not been for the outbreak of the Civil War.[275]

THE BATTLE OF THE HEMP BALES

The Missouri-Kansas border war intensified in the years leading up to the Civil War. In June 1861, Federal forces stationed a garrison in Lexington, Missouri, which occupied a strategic position along the Missouri River. Whoever controlled the town effectively controlled the river. The Federal forces designated the Masonic College their headquarters and reinforced their position.[276]

Major General Stirling Price, commander of the Missouri State Guard, defeated Union forces along the Kansas border at the Battle of Dry Wood Creek in early September. With the border secured, Price turned his attention to Lexington and breaking Union control of the Missouri River.

By the time Price started his march, the Federal garrison in Lexington had been reinforced. On September 10, Colonel James Mulligan with the Twenty-Third Illinois Volunteers arrived to take command of the 3,500 Union troops in Lexington. On the following day, September 11, advanced units of General Price's command totaling more than 7,000 men started to arrive.

The Battle of Lexington, Missouri, aka "The Battle of the Hemp Bales," started on the morning of September 12. Federal troops, behind the cover of some hemp shocks, repelled an advance force of rebel cavalry.[277] Price withdrew his force to regroup and wait for artillery and infantry support. Reinforced, the rebel troops resumed their attack and forced the Federals back to their main defensive position. Price's forces pursued, and another brief engagement ensued. The Union position was formidable, and Price's supply lines were stretched. With the garrison surrounded, Price elected to wait for supplies to reach him, stating, "It is unnecessary to kill off the boys here, patience will give us what we want."[278] The battle resumed on September 18, as the rebels managed to push Federal forces farther into their defensive positions. A nine-hour rebel artillery bombardment followed.[279]

Some of the most violent combat centered on Oliver Anderson's estate home. Federal forces evicted Anderson and converted his home into a field hospital. The rebels believed the home controlled a strategic position. A rebel force commanded by Brigadier General Thomas Harris seized the building during fighting on September 18. Colonel Mulligan considered the attack on the hospital a war crime and ordered Federal troops to retake the home. The Federals succeeded but suffered heavy casualties. The next day, September 19, the rebels recaptured the position.

Hostility between Missouri and Kansas had simmered for years. When the Civil War started, enraged passions resulted in war crimes by both sides. In the Union's eyes, Price's troops attacked and seized a hospital. During their short-lived reoccupation of the house, Federal troops allegedly executed rebel soldiers who attempted to surrender. Both sides accused the other of violating the "Laws of War."[280]

On September 19, the Second Division of State Guard, commanded by Brigadier General Thomas Harris, began to construct movable breastworks, assembled out of hemp bales confiscated from the nearby Anderson warehouses. Rebel soldiers soaked the bales in the Missouri River, making them impervious to incendiary rounds fired from Federal artillery.[281]

The battle's dramatic conclusion started on the morning of September 20. Rebel forces began rolling the hemp bales up the hill toward the Federal position. The waterlogged bales provided perfect cover for advancing rebel forces. Meanwhile, the Union garrison had been under siege for several days without access to water. They were hungry, weak and outnumbered. Price's forces choked off the Federal position and forced their surrender.[282]

By the summer of 1862, Federal forces occupied Missouri and had declared martial law. Oliver Anderson, an outspoken supporter of "the cause," was arrested and imprisoned for suspicion of being part of the "Southern League," a secret group accused of smuggling arms to rebel forces. Anderson still had some important connections in Washington from his time in the military, which he used to help win his release from prison in 1863. Terms of his parole stipulated that Anderson live in the "Northern States" for the duration of the war. He eventually made it back to Lexington, Kentucky, where he lived with his in-laws, the Gratzes, until his death on January 20, 1873.[283]

Hemp in Jessamine County After the Civil War

Jessamine County is bordered by the Kentucky River, and the county's rich, loamy soil has always been productive. It has been asserted that "[p]er acre, no county in the state produces a larger yield." Local farmer Melanchthon Young was considered one of "the great hemp growers of the county and in the last quarter of a century has rarely failed to secure a fine crop."

The introduction of "Chinese hemp seed" in the 1860s is claimed to have "stimulated hemp product." And the productivity of Young's hemp farm "in cultivation for more than one hundred years" is cited as testament to the fertility of Jessamine County soil. In fact, it is claimed that "the yield, after a century of use, of the ground is greater than when the crop was first planted in virgin soil."[284]

Edward Robert "E.R." Sparks

E.R. Sparks (1840–1914) was Jessamine County's most successful hemp industrialist after the Civil War. In Jessamine County, "peak production reached in late 1800s, yielding over 1,000 tons per year, with a value of about $125,000." And E.R. Sparks helped create this lucrative market.

The building at 103 Main Street bears Sparks's name and the date 1881. The building was one of several improvements in which Sparks invested during the late 1800s. In 1871, "he owned a commercial building on Main Street next to the Jessamine Courthouse" and a "hemp and bagging factory…on the opposite side of Main St."[285]

Sparks also invested heavily into improving Nicholasville, albeit often for his own benefit. "His enterprise, coupled with his faith in the future of Nicholasville, and his large investments, both in manufactories and in the laying out of additions and construction of streets and houses, have been greatly instrumental in increasing the population of Nicholasville, and in widening its influence and traffic."[286]

E.R. Sparks building, adjacent to the courthouse in downtown Nicholasville, Kentucky.

Sparks saw the railroad as a way to widen markets for his profitable hemp business. Working with Nicholasville businessman and former mayor John Spear Bronaugh, Sparks and two others successfully created a corridor along the "Riney-B" railroad, which linked Nicholasville to a terminus in Richmond, Kentucky.[287]

Railroads provided direct access to markets to which Kentucky producers had previously been denied. When the railroad in Nicholasville was completed, "All Mr. Sparks had to do to take his product to the train was travel less than one block down Main Street to the train depot or travel up Union Mill Pike [now Richmond Avenue], turn left on Central Avenue, and proceed down the hill to a street named 'Commerce' right next to the tracks."[288]

The project helped improve the profitability of his hemp-manufacturing operation, "which gives employment to a number of hands."[289] Sparks also leveraged his professional success into several elected positions in state and local government, including several terms in the state senate.

Sparks apparently capitalized on the hemp bubble that coincided with the invention of the reaper-binder and the demand for binder twine. His factory on Main Street featured two hackling houses for most years, except 1892,[290] when Sparks dabbled in managing a lumberyard. However, by 1897, he was again running two hackling houses.[291]

By 1903, the Loughridge & Rogers Company had bought Sparks's hemp warehousing operation and was operating three hackling houses. In 1909, the factory was running just one hackling house.[292]

Sparks grew his hemp business in neighboring communities. An 1890 Sanborn fire map shows Sparks expanding an existing facility along the railroad in nearby Lexington.[293]

9

MADISON COUNTY

Madison Hemp and Flax Company

While Madison County has one of the state's most important hemp-related markers, hemp was never central to the county's economy.

Madison county was formed in 1785, and named in honor of James Madison, president of the United States, and lies on the waters of the Kentucky river….Indian corn and tobacco are extensively cultivated, but the hemp and wheat crops are limited to domestic consumption.

The towns of Madison are Richmond and Boonesborough. Richmond the county seat, lies fifty miles from Frankfort. It is a handsome town, with a thriving and intelligent population of 1,000–1,200 souls…a rich and enlightened community—contains…one rope factory.[294]

MADISON FLAX AND HEMP

Began operations here on Silver Creek in 1806. The machinery for spinning hemp and flax was run by water power. In 1808, received permission from the legislature to incorporate and sell stock. Factory produced thread which was sold or used for weaving. One hundred and six spindles were in operation, each capable of spinning daily ½ lb. thread suitable for linen.[295]
—Marker 1362, KY 52, at Silver Creek, marker missing

In 1806, the Kentucky legislature approved the formation of the Madison Flax and Hemp Company, one of the first public companies incorporated in the commonwealth.

The Madison Hemp and Flax Company was a state-of-the-art spinning facility focused on spinning hemp and flax into thread. Five partners started the company: William Macbean; the Maccoun brothers, James and David; Robert Frazier; and aspiring politician Henry Clay. They acquired fifty acres of land along Silver Creek in Madison County in December 1806. The men quickly realized that they required additional capital. Subsequently, in 1808, they petitioned the state legislature for the right to sell one thousand shares of stock at twenty-five dollars a share.[296] This made Madison Hemp and Flax one of Kentucky's first public companies.

Madison Hemp and Flax was a vital link in the supply chain that formed Kentucky's hempire. The factory converted hemp fiber into thread and yarn. In turn, these materials fed the looms of Kentucky's nascent textile and bagging industries.

TATES CREEK MILLS: ELISHA WINTERS & COMPANY

Elisha Winters was already an established hemp merchant in Lexington by the time he opened his general store and mill complex on Tates Creek in Madison County. During the 1790s, when Spain controlled the city and port of New Orleans, Winters established himself as a "great favorite with the Spanish officers," which facilitated his ability to do trade. Winters later opened a ropewalk in New Orleans, where he spun Kentucky hemp into rope.[297]

Elisha Winters and his brother J. Winters first advertised their industrial facility in the December 7, 1793 edition of the *Kentucky Gazette*. The ad stated, "The subscribers continue business in Lexington, as usual," while a new business, "Tates Creek Mills," had just opened. Winters advertised "A LARGE ASSORTMENT of MERCHANDISE…which they will sell on very low terms, for tobacco, Hemp, Wheat, beef, Pork, Hemp feed, Flax," other agricultural produce "or cash." The ad also seeks to "contract (on very generous terms) for the ensuing crop of hemp.[298]

An advertisement in the July 18, 1795 edition of the *Kentucky Gazette* boasts of a new flour mill and continues to "purchase HEMP as usual."[299] However, on October 20, 1795, Elisha Winters issued notice that Winters & Company would be dissolving effective December 1, 1795. The notice sought to collect all outstanding debts.[300]

The following spring, Winters attempted to sell his industrial site. In the March 12, 1796 edition of the *Kentucky Gazette*, he advertised that his business on Tates Creek in Madison County was for sale. It had grown into an impressive integrated industrial site that included a merchant mill, a gristmill, a "saw mill in good repair, and a new hemp mill." He also listed several buildings, including a "two story BRICK HOUSE…a new Framed Dwelling House, kitchen and store house with a number of useful cabins…a ROPE-WALK coverd [*sic*] 250 feet, and may be extended over a level piece of ground 150 fathoms with every apparatus [*sic*] suitable for manufacturing cordage."[301] The grounds also included a distillery and possibly a boatyard.

Elisha Winters invested in many other opportunities to develop central Kentucky. In 1830, he served a controversial term as president of the board of directors of the Lexington & Ohio Railroad. On the board were such notable Lexington businessmen as John Hunt, John Brand, Benjamin Gratz and Henry Clay.[302]

10

HEMP IN MASON COUNTY

The only major hemp producing KY county outside the Blue Grass area. The 1810 crop income was $70,000. Maysville second to only Louisville in finished hemp products, 1830's. Nicholas Arthur factory, using horsepower, was one of several ropewalks, long buildings for spiral winding of hemp fibers. It processed yearly 600,000 lbs of rope worth $41,000.[303]
—Marker 1165, US 68 West, past Maysville Community College

Finding Mason County's hemp marker is a story within a story. Originally dedicated in 1971, at the corner of Second Street and KY 8, the marker disappeared in 1982. To this day, no one knows who took the sign, or why, but it was missing for seven years. In 1989, it mysteriously reappeared at a bus stop near the entrance to Maysville Community College. The sign was rededicated at its current location on US 68 that same year.[304]

Not only does Mason County have a unique hempstory, but Maysville, the county seat, also played a significant role in opening the frontier. Maysville is located on the Ohio River, sixty miles upriver from Cincinnati. Originally named Limestone, it was the territory's most important port during Kentucky's earliest settlement period. Limestone was the gateway into Kentucky. Through its port poured thousands of settlers along with the goods and supplies required to survive and thrive on the frontier. Similarly, Maysville was Kentucky's main port to world markets. By the mid-1840s, Maysville had earned the reputation of being the largest hemp market in the world. Mason County was also home to several pioneering agronomists who conducted field experiments on hemp, planting different seed strains and experimenting with rotting techniques.

LEWIS COLLINS

Lewis Collins (1797–1870) was born at Bryan's Station, outside of Lexington. Orphaned when he was just sixteen, Collins moved to Paris, where he served a printer's apprenticeship under Joel Lyle, editor of the *Paris Citizen.*

Collins moved to Maysville, where served the community in many ways. He was the publisher of the *Maysville Eagle* for over twenty-five years, served as the commissioner of schools for almost two decades and was the first Mason County judge, serving three years starting in 1851.

In 1847, Collins published *Historical Sketches of Kentucky.* Collins was enthralled by Kentucky history, and the volume, which he edited, is a compilation of articles submitted by various contributors. While it was considered the most comprehensive history of Kentucky of its time, it has since been "criticized for its lack of documentation."[305] What Collins did provide was a snapshot of contemporary life in each of the state's counties, including the agricultural and industrial makeup of the towns and communities throughout Kentucky. In the 1840s, when Collins compiled his edition, Kentucky's hemp industry was at its peak.[306] The information about hemp manufacturing and hemp's place in the agricultural and industrial hierarchy is mostly accurate.

In 1877, Richard Collins, Lewis's son, updated and revised *Historical Sketches of Kentucky.* Richard had originally arranged for the commonwealth to adopt the two-volume history as an official textbook in state classrooms. But the state backed out of the agreement, and Collins eventually lost $15,000 fighting the decision in court. About Mason County, Collins wrote:

> *The staple productions are Indian corn, hemp and tobacco. Its agriculture is good and steadily improving; it is probably the most extensive hemp-growing county in the state; and "Mason county tobacco" is famous for its excellence in Europe.*
>
> *Washington was the principal place of trade for a very large scope of country around....At one time it contained fifteen or twenty flourishing mercantile houses; but within the last thirty years it has greatly declined, owing principally to its proximity to the city of Maysville....Washington*

KENTUCKY HISTORIAN

Lewis Collins, 1797-1870, born near Bryan's Station, author of Collins' HISTORICAL SKETCHES OF KENTUCKY. He was presiding judge of Mason County, publisher-editor of the EAGLE, lived here 52 years. His 1847 study of his own state - revised by Richard H. Collins, his son, 1874 as Collins' HISTORY OF KENTUCKY - is considered a basic source for the historian of today.

Lewis Collins Historical Marker, Maysville, Kentucky. Collins's *Historical Sketches of Kentucky*, first published in 1847, was incredibly influential.

is beautifully situated in the heart of a rich and highly cultivated country, three and a half miles from Maysville, and contains...three ropewalks, one of which is in operation.[307]

Mayslick, situated twelve miles from Maysville, on the Lexington turnpike road...contains...rope walk.

Maysville, known for many years as Limestone, from the creek of that name which empties in the Ohio at that place, is situated on the Ohio river, sixty miles above Cincinnati and was named after John May, the owner of the land.

Maysville was incorporated as a city in 1833, is well and compactly built, contains...one large power loom bagging factory with an actual capital paid in of $80,000...five rope-walks.

Maysville is the largest hemp market in the United States and this year her purchases will amount to 6,500 tons. She is the point of reception, storage and transshipment of all merchandise and produce imported and exported by the north-eastern section of Kentucky....As a corporation, she has expended seventy thousand dollars in the construction of the different turnpike roads which concentrate upon her as a terminus.[308]

THE REAL HEMP HIGHWAY

US 68 is one of the main highways connecting Maysville. It was also one of the most significant road projects in American history. Like many roads in

America, US 68 started as a buffalo trace or path through the wilderness. It evolved slowly as commercial traffic increased. In the 1790s, when John Wesley Hunt opened his first general store in Lexington, the journey overland between Maysville to Lexington took up to five days.[309]

Plans to improve the rough trail into a finished road were drawn as early as 1817.[310] But it was the presidential election of 1824 that set the stage for a political feud that influenced the development of one of the nation's most significant roadways. The political landscape in 1824 was dominated by one viable political party, the Democratic-Republicans. In the general election, four candidates were nominated for president. The Democratic-Republican Congressional Caucus nominated Secretary of the Treasury William Crawford as its candidate.

Crawford was wildly unpopular and opposed by three candidates, nominated by their state legislatures. Those candidates were Senator Andrew Jackson of Tennessee, populist "hero" of the Indian Wars and general of the victorious American forces at the Battle of New Orleans; Senator John Quincy Adams of Massachusetts, the son of Founding Father and second president John Adams; and Speaker of the House Kentucky congressman Henry Clay.

The general election was not decided at the ballot box, as none of the candidates earned enough electoral votes to claim victory. Jackson held a slight edge in electoral and popular votes over Adams. Clay and Crawford both finished far behind. Per the Twelfth Amendment, the election was turned over to Congress to decide the victor. In the House of Representatives, Henry Clay played the role of kingmaker, persuading Congress to vote Adams for president. Clay was subsequently rewarded with an appointment as Adams's secretary of state, a position Clay hoped would propel his presidential prospects. Jackson was enraged and accused Clay of subverting the will of the people.[311]

Andrew Jackson significantly defeated Adams in the presidential election of 1828, setting the stage for one of the most bitter policy struggles of the 1830s. Henry Clay's guiding philosophy while he developed the "American System" was that American political independence was inextricably entwined with the nation's economic and industrial development. To develop vital domestic industry, the American System placed tariffs on imported goods from industries deemed critical to the nation. Concurrently, Clay proposed infrastructure improvements to develop domestic industry.

Clay believed that this included the hemp industry. The U.S. Navy had a significant demand for hemp. Russian "Riga reign" was standard in terms

Maysville-Lexington Turnpike marker. A pet project of Senator Henry Clay, the turnpike dramatically cut the time to market for Kentucky hemp.

of price and quality. There were obstacles in getting Kentucky products to markets on the Eastern Seaboard. It cost less to ship hemp to New York and Boston from across the ocean than from Kentucky.

One project near and dear to Clay's heart was the Maysville and Lexington Road Bill. Clay was not a member of the Kentucky congressional caucus when the bill first passed the House of Representatives. Perhaps his influence could have helped it through the Senate, where it failed passage by one vote. In 1830, a second bill, the Maysville Road Bill, was approved by both houses of Congress, only to be vetoed by President Jackson, who had previously indicated his opposition to national funding for internal improvement projects. Jackson believed the turnpike was a "local project" and that, therefore, federal funding for it was unconstitutional.[312]

Regardless of Jackson's position, the project was seen as a sound investment. In 1830, construction of the road began in earnest, incorporating the latest principals in road making. The turnpike was built in five-mile sections. At the end of each section, a tollhouse was erected to help pay for the cost of construction. When completed, the Maysville-Lexington Road covered sixty-five miles and included thirteen tollbooths. More important, travel time from Maysville to Lexington decreased from five days, when John Hunt first traveled from Maysville, to around ten hours.[313]

The road quickly became a vital artery for goods entering and leaving Kentucky, including hemp. Early hemp merchants with access to the Kentucky River had brought their products to market in New Orleans on flatboats. The Maysville-Lexington Road provided central Kentucky manufacturers with direct access to one of the largest hemp markets in the world. Henry Clay himself utilized the turnpike to bring his hemp products to market. One of his sons (Henry Jr. or Thomas A.) wrote to A.M. January & Sons of Maysville about selling some "coils of rope sent with my father's bagging."[314] These events offer proof that the Maysville-Lexington Road was the original "Hemp Highway of Kentucky."

ADAM BEATTY

Mason County resident Adam Beatty was one of Kentucky's leading antebellum agronomists. Born in Hagerstown, Maryland, on May 10, 1777, his family migrated to Kentucky and settled in Lexington in 1800. Adam studied law under Henry Clay's brother-in-law, James Brown. After he was admitted to the bar, Beatty moved to the town of Washington in Mason County, setting up his law practice in 1802.

Beatty held several elected and appointed positions during his early career. He was first elected to the Kentucky legislature in 1809 and commissioned a circuit court judge by Governor Charles Scott in July 1811. Beatty served on the bench for twelve years. He was also elected to the state legislature several times and ran for national office.

When Beatty retired from the judiciary in 1823, he turned his full attention to his farm. Beatty explored ways of improving agriculture, immersing himself in the latest American and foreign literature and establishing himself as one of the leading agronomists in Kentucky. He later served as president of the Maysville Agricultural Society and as vice-president to the Kentucky chapter.[315]

Beatty was also an early and eager contributor to the "agricultural" press. He regularly contributed to the *Kentucky Farmer*, where his essays were later compiled into a book. In 1841, Adam Beatty authored four award-winning essays for the Kentucky Agricultural Society's annual exposition. His entries included the essay "On the Cultivation of Hemp." Each winning essay earned Beatty a "premium" of twenty dollars.[316]

In addition to his agricultural research, Beatty was also active in protecting Kentucky producers. He established a relationship with Henry Clay and was a vocal supporter of Clay's proposed tariffs on imported hemp.

Beatty was not the only farmer in Mason County who experimented with hemp. On a trip to France in 1851, L. Maltby was introduced to So-na, or Chinese hemp. Maltby arranged to bring seeds back to Kentucky. In 1852, he and C.A. Marshall experimented with the new strain. The French growing season is shorter than Kentucky's. In France, the plant grew tall and produced excellent fiber, but the season was not long enough to allow the seeds to mature. French hemp producers established seed plantations in Algiers, North Africa. The seed was then imported into France and grown for fiber. Maltby and Marshall originally believed that they had to replicate this model, growing seed in Louisiana and the fiber crop in Kentucky. To their delight, they discovered that the strain produced larger yields of higher quality fiber than had the legacy heirloom strains they had previously grown. More important, the seed planted in Kentucky had fully matured by harvest.[317]

Hemp Manufacturing

The port at Maysville made the town a logical hemp-manufacturing site. Boatyards in Maysville required rigging and caulking. The freight business associated with the port also required access to rope and cordage. Bagging factories supplied materials for local businesses and for the cotton plantations downriver. By 1845, Maysville had one of the most extensive hemp markets in the Union.[318]

Michael Ryan

Michael Ryan (1802–1879) was the son of Irish immigrants. Born in Maysville, he prospered as a grain dealer and hemp merchant. When he married Maria Richeson in 1841, he was considered the largest hemp dealer in the area and one of the largest in Kentucky. The couple soon began work on their home, which they named Riverside. Completed in 1845, the house at 716 West Second Street has a breathtaking view of the Ohio River. Michael was an accomplished musician on the flute, coronet and violin. "Often, when a storm was coming up the river, he would be seen on the porch of his house, letting the storm play an accompaniment to his flute."

Among his other business interests, Ryan was the principal investor in the Maysville and Big Sandy Railroad, which was later acquired by the Chesapeake and Ohio Railroad. Some of the original railroad infrastructure built by Ryan remains in service today.

Michael Ryan's most important contribution to the community was in people. He was one of Maysville's thirty-two "emancipators." This group of wealthy, respected citizens took out loans to purchase enslaved people. They then paid that enslaved person a wage with which he or she could purchase their own freedom. The work of the emancipators contributed to the increasing population of free Blacks in Mason County prior to the Civil War.[319]

After Ryan died, his house was purchased by Henry E. Pogue, who owned a large distillery. The home remained in the Pogue family until 1955.

HEMP IN SCOTT COUNTY

Rev. Elijah Craig established at Georgetown, in 1789, one of the earliest ropewalks, which were long sheds for spiral winding of hemp fibers. Also started fulling mill 1793. Both factories made cordage and rigging for vessels built on the Ohio and Kentucky Rivers. Peak production in 1839; over 1,000 tons processed yearly with a value of $120,000.[320]
—Marker 1166, US 25, north of Georgetown, north lawn of the Cardome Center

Scott county was formed in 1792, and named in honor of Governor Charles Scott.

The southern and south-eastern portion…is embraced in that beautiful region known as the "Garden of Kentucky"…unsurpassed in fertility.

Hemp and corn are staple crops and wheat is cultivated to some extent.

Georgetown, the seat of justice…contains…2 woollen [sic] manufactories, two carding factories, two bagging and rope factories.[321]

ELIJAH CRAIG

The history and hempstory of the Scott County seat, Georgetown, literally start with the Reverend Elijah Craig (1738 or 1743–1808). Craig, a Baptist preacher in Virginia, was imprisoned for preaching without a license from the Anglican Church. Craig's resulting passion for religious freedom steered him into politics. In the 1770s, he served as a legislative liaison, where he subsequently worked with both James Madison and Patrick Henry.

The Craig-Hawkins party migrated to Kentucky around 1782. After surviving the Siege of Bryan's Station, they settled a prime spot in central Kentucky near Royal Springs. Here, Craig set about building his "city set on a hill." The town was originally commissioned as Lebanon in 1784. However, in 1790, Craig petitioned the Virginia legislature to rename the community Georgetown, in honor of George Washington.[322]

Georgetown is the product of Craig's vision. He laid out the streets of downtown and built several of the first institutions. In 1787, Craig established the first classical school in Kentucky and later started the Rittenhouse Academy. Georgetown College, the first Baptist College west of the Allegheny Mountains, was established on land donated by Elijah Craig. In 1789, he established a distillery and later staked a claim as the creator of bourbon whiskey.[323]

Craig was also the founder of Port William (Carrollton), where he "dominated the Kentucky River upstream keelboat trade. In 1795, he built a warehouse at the mouth of the Kentucky River and advertised [rates for going up stream]."[324]

"The first ropewalk in Georgetown was established by Elijah Craig in 1793."[325] He opened a second ropewalk in 1798 near Frankfort on the Kentucky River.[326] The ropewalks supplied cordage and rigging to area boatyards, while the fulling mill tightened the weave and finished textiles prior to their manufacture into other goods.

THE FIRST PAPER MILL IN THE WEST

Craig also operated the first paper mill on the frontier. Big Spring Branch was considered an ideal location. "The largest spring in Kentucky, with a fall of 15 feet in less than a mile, could well turn the wheel to churn rags and *hemp* tow into pulp and offers a constant supply of clean, sparkling water."[327] Craig started construction on the mill in 1792 and purchased papermaking "moulds from John Seller of Pennsylvania."[328] In March 1793, Craig and his partners, James and Alexander Parker of Lexington, announced in the *Kentucky Gazette* that their paper mill was operating. Elijah Craig's grandson Elijah Grant took over running the mill in 1808. He sold it in 1811, and the mill changed hands several times before it burned down in 1836 or 1837.[329]

Until the development of wood pulp paper in 1867, most paper was manufactured from discarded clothes and rags and was called "rag paper." On the frontier, "hemp…went into the manufacture of the homespun used as clothing for slaves, and in the form of 'Kentucky jeans.'"[330] Craig's paper likely had significant hemp content. Prior to the Civil War, cotton clothing was not widely worn. The southern states exported raw cotton fiber to Europe, where the fiber was spun and manufactured into textiles. These textiles were then imported into the United States from Europe. Imported textiles were expensive, and cotton clothes were worn almost exclusively by the rich.[331] In Kentucky, hempen textiles were preferred for agricultural bagging and for clothing for agricultural workers and enslaved people.

Elijah Craig's death created confusion in Georgetown. Where did Craig's personal vision end and the town begin? Craig claimed land, built a business and made infrastructure improvements such as culverts and a bridge at Royal Spring. But Craig had not officially claimed specific land, and the city had paid for some of the improvements. As a result, the Kentucky legislature ordered an official survey of Georgetown in 1816.[332]

Craig's son-in-law Josiah Pitts was named the main heir for much of Elijah Craig's land.[333] Pitts had moved to Kentucky from Virginia around 1805 and married Craig's daughter Lucy. Pitts was a very successful and influential merchant in Georgetown. "He embarked largely in trade purchasing all the tobacco, wheat and flour, hemp bagging cordage… not only in the county, but in the neighboring regions."[334] These goods were floated downriver on flatboats to New Orleans, and the profits were invested in goods needed in Kentucky.

THE HEMP HOUSES OF GEORGETOWN

Georgetown had a rich hemp culture that included cultivation, processing and manufacturing. Its downtown area features several homes built by people whose wealth was in large part generated by the hemp industry. Many of these homes line Main Street and represent several different eras and styles of architecture, making a walk around downtown Georgetown fascinating.

THE LEOPOLD TARLETON HOUSE, 336 EAST MAIN STREET

Leo Tarleton's house was originally the center of a substantial hemp industrial site. The original lot, developed before Georgetown College acquired a portion of it, would have backed up to "ropewalk alley." The property was purchased and developed in the 1820s by Leopold "Leo" Tarleton (1794–1867). Not only was the home the site of one of the city's earliest hemp manufactories, but Leo Tarleton was also descended from one of Scott County's earliest settlers, Jeremiah "the Catholic" Tarleton (1755–1826).[335]

At the outbreak of the Revolutionary War, Jeremiah Tarleton enlisted in Maryland's Fifth Independent Company, serving until 1780. Originally organized to protect Chesapeake Bay, the unit saw combat in New York and New Jersey throughout 1776 and 1777. Tarleton participated in several major engagements, including the Battle of Monmouth in 1778.

Jeremiah returned to Maryland when his commitment ended and there married Elizabeth Medley in 1782. In the late 1780s, the Tarleton family joined a party that migrated from Maryland to Kentucky. Jeremiah emerged as one of the leaders of the group, helping lead them to an area just west of Georgetown, White Sulphur.[336]

Jeremiah's son Leopold (1794–1867) married Mary Ann Breckinridge (1802–1841) in 1819 and moved to Georgetown shortly after. Construction of his home started around 1820 as the center of an industrial site. Tarleton operated two ropewalks on the property, one adjacent to his home and the other located at the intersection of College and Mulberry Streets. The property also included a "brick 'hemp-house'," which likely served as a finished goods warehouse.

Tarleton operated the factory site until 1844, when he sold the property to Levi Prewitt for $6,500. Leo Tarleton and his second wife eventually attempted to relocate to Louisiana, where Tarleton invested in sugar plantations and enslaved people. The Civil War destroyed his property and wiped him out financially. After the war, Leo returned to Kentucky, where he died in 1867.[337]

Tarleton's first wife, Mary Ann, is buried in a small family graveyard behind the house, located on adjacent property now owned by Georgetown College.

THE PRESIDENT'S HOUSE, 444 EAST MAIN STREET

The President's House was built by Harvey Cloud Graves (1804–1885) in 1859. Graves purchased two adjoining lots on Main Street on which he built his home. He was "one of the wealthiest hemp growers in Central Kentucky" and often called the "largest hemp grower in this part of the country."

Showing the influence of the hemp industry in central Kentucky, this rope motif window molding adorns 618 East Main Street, Georgetown, Kentucky.

618 East Main Street, Georgetown, Kentucky. The window molding motif suggests a hemp connection.

Graves was considered a civic-minded man who "made the world better for his having lived in it." He contributed to several major projects, including helping establish Georgetown College and founding the Farmer's Bank of Georgetown. Graves identified as "a Union Democrat during the Civil War, a unique role for a Scott County hemp grower." His politics and demeanor caused him to become known as the "benevolent Yankee" who "stood by the Union when the prevailing mood in Georgetown was that of the Confederacy." Graves worked to enhance his local reputation, and "his generosity towards impoverished Confederates became almost legendary."

In 1961, the house was sold to Georgetown College and today fittingly serves as the home for the president of the college.[338]

THE HAWKINS HOUSE, 324 EAST JACKSON STREET

The Hawkins family and the Craigs traveled together from Virginia to Kentucky. They were related by marriage, much like the Boones and Bryans. Mary Hawkins Craig, Elijah Craig's mother, was one of the female heroes of the Siege of Bryan's Station.

Fire devastated the Scott County clerk's office twice in the early 1800s (1814 and 1837). These fires destroyed or damaged Georgetown's earliest records. Most accounts agree that Thomas Hawkins was deeded the property in 1815 and established a ropewalk and one of Georgetown's first bagging factories behind the home. Jackson Street, which runs parallel to Main Street, eventually earned the nickname "ropewalk alley," as it developed into a hub of hemp manufacturing in the early 1800s.

In 1826, Thomas Hawkins sold the home and factory for $1,900. It sold again before the lot was acquired by the Kentucky Baptist Education Society (KBES) for Georgetown College in August 1830. However, in 1831, the college was deeded a better location, and by 1834, the lot was again in private hands and the hemp factory back in operation. Various ownership groups operated the ropewalk and bagging factory until 1848, when it was converted into a private residence.[339]

The property was sold in 1858 and used for educational purposes until 1939, when it again reverted to a private residence.[340] The large backyard, visible from nearby Hollyhock Lane, provides insight into the scale of a ropewalk.

Frontier homes like Thomas Hawkins's house developed over time. The west wing of the home appears to be the oldest. Architectural details, such as the freestanding chimney and simple fireplace mantle, suggest that this section of the home was built around 1790, before Hawkins acquired the property. Hawkins likely expanded the home as the profitability of the hemp factory allowed.[341]

E.N. Offutt Hemp Warehouse

Appearing on the 1886 Sanborn map of Georgetown was a business identified as the "Hemp Fact'y E.N. Offutt & Co."[342] located at the end of Jackson Street. This was the E.N. Offutt Hemp Warehouse. The business included a brick warehouse, with a wood frame hackling house located behind the main building, and a small brick office to the east.

The 1890 the Sanborn map showed that Offutt's business had expanded significantly, with the addition of a brick warehouse on Maddox Avenue. Called the "E.N. Offutt & Co Hemp, Grain & Seed W. Ho," the new building also included a rail spur terminating in back of the warehouse.[343] The addition coincided with the increased demand for hemp by the binder twine industry.

The 1895 map shows continued growth at the Offutt property. The "E.N. Offutt & Co. Elevator"[344] now operated across the rail spur from the hemp, grain and seed warehouse. The company also added a coal warehouse.

Seed warehouse of Ezra N. Offutt, built in the late 1800s, Georgetown, Kentucky.

By 1907, the Sanborn map shows that E.N. Offutt had taken on a partner and dropped hemp from his business completely. "Offutt and Blackburn" pivoted toward the agricultural supply business. The original hemp warehouse was converted into a "Ware Ho. Agric't Implements-Hay Grain, etc.," while the more recent hemp, seed and grain warehouse now specialized in "Feed."[345]

The factory was owned and operated by Ezra Nelson Offutt (1843–1911). Offutt's grandfather Alexander Offutt (1767–1823) moved from Maryland to Kentucky in 1810. Ezra Nelson Offutt died in his home on East Main Street in Georgetown in 1911.[346]

BLUEGRASS CORDAGE COMPANY AND THE BINDER TWINE BUBBLE

With the introduction of the mass-produced reaper-binder in 1880, the demand for high-quality binder twine exploded. This resulted in fresh interest and investment in Kentucky's hemp industry. In 1870, there were nine cordage factories in Kentucky, and by 1880, a twine factory in Lexington had closed. But by 1890, fueled by the demand for binder twine, sixteen cordage factories were operating in Kentucky. The binder twine bubble popped quicker than it had inflated, and by 1900, only six cordage mills operated in Kentucky. By 1919, only four cordage factories remained.[347]

Bluegrass Cordage Company, Georgetown, Kentucky, built during the binder twine boom. The firm went out of business in less than five years.

The short-lived Bluegrass Cordage Company started and closed within this brief window. It had a promising start. "Over $100,000 was raised in 1888 for the erection of a twine factory in Georgetown…and stockholders twice sent William Fleming to Scotland to purchase what was thought to be the best machinery available."[348]

But around the same time that Bluegrass Cordage Company opened, one of the nation's first trusts attempted to monopolize the market for binder twine. At the dawn of the 1880s, four eastern cordage companies formed a trust called the National Cordage Association in an attempt to stabilize the cordage market. Their efforts, while initially successful, fueled a speculative bubble that distorted the demand for hemp and crashed the entire stock market. The fate of the Bluegrass Cordage Company, which opened during the height of this bubble, was at the mercy of market forces it could not have seen coming or have understood if it had. The rise and fall of the National Cordage Company and its successors is a cautionary tale about speculating in developing markets.

THE NATIONAL CORDAGE COMPANY AND THE PANIC OF 1893

Trade alliances in the cordage industry had been attempted as early as 1861. Cordage manufacturers attempted to "establish certain customs in trade, correct abuses and misbranding and to come to an understanding regarding pricing."[349] These alliances were doomed to fail, in part because the agreements didn't create mechanisms for identifying and punishing violators. Members violated the agreement as it suited their individual businesses.[350] Additionally, geography meant that certain manufacturers were able to communicate with each other better, which resulted in their wielding disproportionate influence.

Rules changed and financial penalties instituted for violators, but the revisions were no deterrent and just as difficult to enforce. Alliance members continued to operate in the immediate interests of their own businesses. In 1878, cordage manufacturers attempted to create a "pool." This model essentially forecast annual cordage requirements and assigned a percentage of the manufacturing to member businesses. Still, business owners continued to prioritize their own profits.[351]

In the early 1880s, following the collapse of the "pool system," four of the largest cordage manufacturers—L. Waterbury Company, the Tucker and

Carter Cordage Company, William Wall's and Sons and the Elizabethport Cordage Company—formed a "trust" called the National Cordage Association. The trust created a mechanism that allowed these companies to leverage their manufacturing capacity to negotiate the best raw material and sales prices. Members still operated their factories independently, but they had the advantage of knowing that their material costs and sales price were stable.[352]

The model was very successful, but the National Cordage Association trust was structured like the Standard Oil Trust. Standard Oil had recently captured the attention of federal banking regulators, whose investigations resulted in the Sherman Antitrust Act of 1890.

Fearing increased federal attention, attorneys for the National Cordage Association created the National Cordage Corporation in 1887. NCC was created as a joint venture functioning as the purchasing and sales organization for the four factories involved. To capitalize the company, the four member businesses leased their manufacturing facilities from NCC. They each paid National Cordage $375,000 to lease their factories for ninety-nine years.[353]

This working capital provided the liquidity required to operate a seasonal business of this scale. And while the individual firms stuck to their business models, by leveraging their combined capacity, National Cordage was very profitable. From 1887 to 1890, National Cordage was privately held and the business model functioned as designed.[354]

In 1890, National Cordage Association formally disbanded the trust and the National Cordage Company went public. Flush with cash from the public stock offering, the board of directors changed the business model and embarked on a three-point plan to monopolize the binder twine market. This included cornering the market on raw materials, acquiring the competition to expand production capacity and controlling the manufacture of "spinning" equipment.[355]

The new goal led to the collapse of the company and sent shockwaves through the stock market. Initially, the National Cordage Corporation used its established network of raw fiber suppliers and leveraged its combined material demand to lock in low contract pricing. Lower material cost allowed NCC to offer lower finished goods prices, and they flourished.

National Cordage's attempt to corner the fiber market changed its procurement philosophy. NCC no longer leveraged its known demand to secure the lowest possible price; it now set the top price for fiber by attempting to purchase all available material. NCC initially focused on

After hemp is sufficiently rotted, or "retted," it is "shocked" to prevent further rot. Shown here is shocked hemp in a Kentucky hemp field.

purchasing imported fibers like sisal, abaca and jute. When its competitors sourced alternative materials, like Kentucky hemp, National Cordage bought that as well. Farmers responded to increased demand and better prices by planting more acreage. In the late 1800s, Kentucky farmers led the nation in hemp production.

By 1891, National Cordage even went so far as to create a "National Syndicate." Throughout 1891, buyers from "the syndicate" purchased very large quantities of hemp for future delivery, recording transactions in a "small black book without a name."[356] National Cordage continued this strategy in 1892 and attempted to corner the supply of sisal, the preferred material for binder twine.

National Cordage's attempt to corner the hemp market backfired. Instead of leveraging its combined demand to secure the lowest price, NCC was committed to purchase tons of fiber at prices it had artificially inflated. Higher material prices resulted in production costs that exceeded the sale price of twine, resulting in huge losses.[357]

The second part of National Cordage's plan to monopolize the binder twine market was expansion and growth thru acquisition.

NCC's first round of acquisition and expansion was fueled by the revenue generated when the board of directors took the company public. Flush with cash from the public stock offering, National Cordage bought ten spinning mills. This gave NCC "control over something like forty percent of the rope and twine production of the country."[358] However, in many instances, the mills it acquired were overvalued, and at least two of the mills the company purchased were closed after their acquisition.[359]

While the attempt to corner the market on raw material had created losses for NCC, it also created acquisition opportunities. Competitors who experienced trouble obtaining raw materials were targeted for acquisition.[360] National Cordage often overpaid for the assets it acquired.[361] Furthermore, due to weak no-compete agreements, it sometimes ended up in a game of industrial "whack-a-mole." The former owners of a factory just acquired by NCC would find a business partner to be the front man for a new factory, and windfall profits were invested in new factories with modern equipment.[362] By January 1892, either through acquisition or lease, NCC could claim it controlled approximately 90 percent of the nation's rope and twine production capacity.[363]

The final part of National Cordage's attempt to corner the binder twine industry was to control the distribution of manufacturing equipment. NCC entered into a series of contracts and agreements with equipment manufacturers in the United States and England.[364] These agreements gave National Cordage the exclusive rights to market equipment. If a company wanted to purchase the latest spinning machines, they had to agree to use the equipment in support of business National Cordage placed with them. NCC even paid one competitor, "Good Companies $200,000 annually not to make cordage or sell equipment to other mills."[365]

The directors of NCC took an undisciplined approach toward monopolizing the market for binder twine. Instead of growing its share of the market by investing in new equipment, improving efficiency and strategic expansion, NCC tried to buy everything: raw materials, the competition, even distribution rights for new equipment. As a result, NCC squandered its cash on overpriced raw materials and obsolete mills filled with inefficient equipment.

Part of the problem was the greed created when the company went public. "When, however, two executives of the company became more interested in the market quotation of their stocks than in the wise administration of their cordage mills, the enterprise was changed from a business to a speculation."[366] This dovetailed with a general opinion among the investing community that "through a nominal control over the country's production of cordage the National Cordage Company could exert a monopolistic influence on prices and also secure great profits from the economies of large scale production."[367]

NCC built a house of cards doomed to fall. It had taken loans and offered stock based on inventory assets valued at their manufacturing costs and manufacturing capacity as opposed to the actual value of the company. The company held roughly $4 million in assets but it was capitalized at $15 million and expected to pay dividends.[368]

The walls started to collapse in April 1893. National Cordage had secured loans against its finished goods inventory. These were mostly "demand loans and short-term commercial paper."[369] Shortly after NCC secured this capital, the first tremors of the Panic of 1893 were felt when Reading Railroad defaulted on its loans. Between the failure of the Reading and what was called the "free silver controversy," creditors became nervous. National Cordage was informed that its loans would not be extended.

On April 28, 1893, a Friday, shares of NCC preferred stock were trading at $103.75, while common shares traded at $61.00 per share. That Saturday, April 30, the board of directors announced that it would issue $2.5 million to investors in the form of a stock split. Previously, such a move had inspired investor confidence and netted NCC fresh investors. This time, it had the opposite effect. Factored in with other concerning market forces, the move caused National Cordage shares to plummet when the stock market opened for trading on Monday, May 1. By the closing bell the following Friday, NCC shares were trading at $18.75 per share common; $65.20 a share preferred. The collapse of NCC created a ripple effect; three brokerage houses were forced to close during the sell-off. The panic caused other stocks to fall as well, with shares of General Electric dropping from $84 to $58 a share in one day.[370]

The failure of National Cordage transformed the binder twine industry. William Deering and Company, one of the manufacturers of reaper-binders, was contracted with NCC to supply twine. When National Cordage collapsed, it failed to make delivery on those contracts. William Deering and Company responded by opening its own cordage and twine mills and making its warranty contingent on farmers using its branded twine. McCormick, the other major reaper-binder manufacturer, quickly emulated this model.[371] These moves effectively ended the binder twine boom that had fueled the Kentucky hemp industry at the end of the nineteenth century.

IMPACT ON BLUEGRASS CORDAGE COMPANY

Bluegrass Cordage Company (BCC) began operations at the height of the binder twine boom. National Cordage's attempt to corner the market for imported raw materials created an ideal situation for a company like Bluegrass Cordage, which initially focused on making twine from Kentucky hemp. When NCC attempted to control both the domestic and imported supply of fiber, Kentucky farmers responded to rising fiber prices by planting more hemp. The twine manufacturers on the Eastern Seaboard were more directly impacted by the rising cost and scarce availability of abaca (manilla hemp), jute and sisal. Their costs were going up, or they were unable to meet orders. Kentucky manufacturers, meanwhile, were close to a source of raw fiber and their customers in the Midwest. BCC started operations during the height of this bubble.

The Panic of 1893, the financial crisis created in part by the collapse of National Cordage, was the nation's largest economic depression to date.[372] Its repercussions rippled through markets across the country. Freed of the artificial forces of National Cordage's attempt to corner the fiber market, the price of raw materials plummeted. Imported fibers, particularly sisal, were now widely available to the twine mills on the Eastern Seaboard. The flood of imported fibers caused domestic hemp prices to fall. Additionally, NCC had converted a significant amount of its raw material into twine and rope. The company was forced to liquidate this inventory below cost to maintain cash flow, further collapsing the binder twine market.

In 1894, the Senate Finance Committee held hearings to discuss tariffs on imported fibers and textiles. As part of its investigation, the committee issued a "Circular Letter of Inquiry" to companies engaged in potentially impacted industries. The letter sought the input of manufacturers concerning the recent economic collapse. The letter included thirty-five questions, including those concerning general information used to classify each business by industry type, size and location; census-type questions about employment levels, wages and working hours; and questions about the direct impact on business of the current economic crisis. The questionnaire also gave respondents an opportunity to voice their opinion about the causes of the crisis and suggest changes to tariff rates or applicable custom laws. There were also several questions pertaining to raw materials used in the fabrication of products and the impact of raising or lowering applicable tariffs on those materials.[373]

Bluegrass Cordage's response confirmed that the factory had been running at half capacity since July 1893 because of a "reduction in orders."

The company attributed the slowdown to "precautions against extended credit, and fears from Congressional action." When later asked to elucidate on the causes of the "present depression" and suggest a possible "remedy," Bluegrass Cordage offered a rambling response, only vaguely alluding to the collapse of National Cordage. "The cause of the present depression is pension legislation, swamping the Treasury surplus, giving speculative bankers a basis for methods leading to distrust, following a 'booming' tendency, in connection with some foreign complications. We think matters would have righted themselves after Congressional action on the Sherman bill, had the country not feared tariff agitation."[374]

The pension legislation, passed during the Republican administration of Benjamin Harrison, provided pensions for veterans (Union soldiers) of the Civil War. By 1894, these pensions accounted for approximately 37 percent of the federal budget. However, when the pension act was passed in 1888, the government operated at a surplus in part fueled by tariffs on things like imported fibers. The comment about "speculative bankers," while vague, was perhaps an allusion to the collapse of National Cordage in 1893. The "boom" period undoubtedly referred to the artificial bubble created by NCC's attempt to corner the binder twine market. The "foreign complications" mentioned also possibly referred to raw material acquisition. The Sherman Antitrust Act, enacted in 1890, had been anticipated by the National Cordage Alliance and motivated it to incorporate into the National Cordage Company in 1887.

The final survey question solicited input for changes to "existing rates of duty or administrative customs laws." The reply from Bluegrass Cordage was short and defiant: "We desire nothing that the Democratic party can or will indorse [sic], other than to hope for a speedy conclusion of the entire matter."[375]

Bluegrass Cordage's response to the congressional "Circular Letter of Inquiry" suggests that management misread the prevailing economic climate. BCC failed to understand the causes of the depression and had no plan to emerge. While its response showed that the sale price of its products dropped 25 percent in the four years since it opened its factory, it showed no awareness of the market factors that created the price drop. Management in part blamed the depression on the Republican-backed Dependent and Disability Pension Act while later disparagingly dismissing any potential relief from a Democratic administration. The market manipulation and failure of National Cordage barely earned a veiled mention.

Sanborn fire maps of Georgetown indicate that by 1895 Bluegrass Cordage was closed. The shareholders still met regularly to approve the sale of land parcels. These transactions were reported in the *Georgetown Times* through the early 1900s.

One final incident, reported in the May 4, 1904 edition of the *Georgetown Times*, suggests that management issues likely contributed to the company's failure. That March, former factory superintendent William Fleming was discovered hiding in a twine factory in Albany, New York. Arrested, Fleming confessed to several other instances of industrial espionage.[376]

The remaining buildings were purchased and converted into a feed and farm supply store. During World War II, the feed mill distributed hemp seed for the Commodity Credit Corporation's "Hemp for Victory" program.

Today, the former Bluegrass Cordage Company building is occupied by Hilander Feed, an agricultural supply store. Located at 618 Military Street, Hilander Feed features an eclectic collection of historic artifacts.

HEMP IN SHELBY COUNTY

S helby County is adjacent to Jefferson County. The county seat, Shelbyville, is only about thirty-five miles from Louisville. The county is relatively landlocked.

Shelby county was formed in 1792, and named in honor of governor Isaac Shelby. The soil is…remarkably fertile. The grasses succeed well; but hemp, corn and wheat, form the staple products; horses, mules, cattle, hogs, bagging and bale rope, the principal articles of export.[377]

A MISSING MARKER

One of the chief producing counties. Crop income reached a yearly high of $150,000 in 1860. Nine hundred tons of hemp were consumed to produce 2,000 bales of twine and 5,000 coils of rope this same year. One of the ten Bluegrass counties which accounted for more than 90 percent of the yield of the whole country in the late 1800's.[378]
—*Marker 1320, US 60 at KY 714, Hempridge Road, marker missing*

The text of the marker focuses on the value of the 1860 hemp crop and Shelby County's contribution to Kentucky's overall nation-leading yield in the late 1800s. The marker was located at the terminal end of Hempridge Road because of the amount of hemp raised in the area.

Top: Hempridge Baptist Church, built in 1916, Shelby County. Formed in 1913, the congregation is still active today.

Bottom: The ghosts of Hempridge Road, where the hemp once grew tall and lush. Shelby County, Kentucky.

A claim from an article in the *Louisville Courier-Journal* asserts that a farmer raised a hemp plant so large the harvested stalk was made into a cane by Will Waddy and presented to Senator Henry Clay. Clay then exclaimed that an area that could produce such a fine hemp stalk ought to be called "Hempridge." It is claimed that Clay later put the cane on exhibit at the Smithsonian Institute in Washington.[379]

As the name implies, Hempridge Road winds along the top of a ridge, with farms dotting either side. Some of the farms are still active, many are not. In 1913, a new congregation formed among the residents of Hempridge. By 1916, they had collected enough money to erect the Hempridge Baptist Church at the top of the rise.

But the good times were fleeting, like they always seem to be with hemp. Slowly, the vibrant farms that dotted the countryside started to fade, leaving the ghosts of Hempridge Road.

ROWLETT RICE

Rowlett Rice moved from Virginia to Kentucky following the Revolutionary War, settling near Clay Village in Shelby County. There, he started a farm that mainly "produced hemp and flax."[380] He also worked as a carpenter. Rowlett was working on a house when he fell and injured his head. He never fully recovered. His youngest son, Anderson (1810–1867), took care of his father and the family farm until he married and moved to Spencer County, where he was very successful.[381]

WILLIAM SLEADD HOUSE

Ezra Sleadd was an early settler in Shelby County, arriving after the Revolutionary War. He established a two-thousand-acre plantation near Hooper in Shelby County on which hemp was one of the major crops. The original log home he built was replaced with a Greek Revival home by his son William between 1858 and 1860.[382] The property, at 3980 Hooper Station Road, remained in the Sleadd family for over 110 years.

SHELBY VANNATTA AND JOHN P. ALLEN

Shelby VanNatta (1820–1893) dabbled briefly in Shelby County hemp manufacturing in the 1850s. When Shelby was sixteen, he clerked at a store in Clay Village. He moved to Shelbyville in 1840 and opened a dry goods store.[383] Shelby did well and briefly was partners with John P. Allen and E. Hickman in a ropewalk. Shelby sold his interest to Allen in 1856,[384] around the same time that he accepted a banking position.

John P. Allen Sr. was an early settler in Shelby County. He "engaged in many enterprises in which he [was] successful. He was engaged for many years in the manufacture of hemp."[385]

Throughout Kentucky, "from 1815–1820 the manufacture of bale rope and bagging in Kentucky was not profitable to most of the smaller establishments."[386] This impacted Shelby County, where "White and Castleman, proprietors of a bagging factory located on the Tick Creek... suspended operations and explained that the price of bagging was low because of 'Urope being able to furnish said article much cheaper than it could be produced in America."[387]

During this period, some factories managed to stay in business by focusing on products consumed on local farms. For example, "John and James Bradshaw of Shelbyville provided yarns, bale rope, bed cords, plow lines, twine, etc., but said their output was far short of capacity."[388]

13

WOODFORD COUNTY HEMP

Woodford county, the last of the nine counties organized by Virginia, was formed in 1788, and named after Gen. William Woodford. It is situated in the heart of the state....

The farms are large...and in a high state of cultivation; the population intelligent, refined and independent. Hemp, corn, oats and wheat are the staple products; horses, mules, cattle, hogs, bagging and bale rope, the principal exports.

Versailles, the seat of justice of Woodford...is a beautiful, and thriving town with...eight bagging factories....[It was] [e]stablished in 1792, and named after the city of Versailles in France.

Midway...a handsome village, situated on the Lexington rail road... has...3 hemp factories.

Mortonsville...also a neat village, situated four miles south of Versailles... contains...one bagging factory.[389]

THE KENTUCKY-ILLINOIS HEMP COMPANY

One of the chief producing counties, crop income reached a yearly high of $125,000 in the 1840s. During these peak years, there were 19 ropewalks, long sheds for spiral winding of hemp fibers. In 1941, Kentucky-Illinois Hemp Co. built a breaking plant at Versailles, with 2,000 acres of hemp under contract, using 4 binders and 16 reapers to harvest crop.[390]

—Marker 1167, US 60, one mile east of Versailles

Hemp warehouse, Midway, Kentucky. Hemp/railroad entrepreneur Benjamin Gratz was instrumental in establishing Midway. In 1864, Midway shipped 636,000 pounds of hemp. *Information on hemp shipments is from William Penn, The Civil War in Midway, Kentucky (Midway, KY: Historic Midway Museum, 2012).*

The "Woodford County Hemp" roadside marker is an example of providing just enough information to create confusion. Considering the diplomatic landscape of the 1940s, it is easy to assume that the Kentucky-Illinois Hemp Company had its roots in venture capitalists. In 1940, hemp fiber was still used in many commercial applications and remained a critical material of war. As war engulfed the nations of Europe and Asia, it drove increased demand for hemp and hempen goods both in the United States and abroad.

But, the hempstory behind the Kentucky-Illinois Hemp Company is far more interesting and complex than venture capitalists exploiting global war. The company is where Kentucky's hempstory intersects with the "New Billion Dollar Crop." The narrative starts in Illinois much earlier than 1940, with a nascent science called "chemurgy."

CHEMURGY

Chemurgy was a branch of chemistry now called biomechanical engineering. The word *chemurgy* was first popularized by chemist William Jay Hale (1876–1955), the director of organic chemistry research at Dow Chemical from 1919 to 1934. Hale laid out his vision for this new science in his book *The Farm Chemurgic*, first published in 1934. Chemurgy explored ways to convert agricultural biomass (plants) into a variety of industrial materials.

George Washington Carver (1864–1943), best known for his research on peanuts, was another of chemurgy's founders and most ardent supporters. Carver, Hale and other scientists believed that the farm, specifically agricultural waste, could be the source of raw materials that would fuel an agriculture-powered industrial renaissance. Their work captured the attention of manufacturing innovator Henry Ford, who saw in their research the potential to grow automobiles.

To further this vision and advance the research of Hale, Carver and others, Henry Ford helped establish the Farm Chemurgic Council in 1935. Cellulose was identified as a promising substance, a versatile material adaptable to a variety of applications that held the key to unlocking a manufacturing revolution. Research into cellulose explored its suitability as the base material for products like paper and plastics.[391] Movie film and cellophane are examples of cellulose-based plastics.

The principals of chemurgy were not new. In 1916, in USDA *Bulletin 404*, "Hemp Hurds as Paper Making Material" reported on experiments into the use of hemp "hurds" (cellulose) as a potential replacement for pulped poplar logs in papermaking. The two-part report noted that while an acre of hemp produced significantly more cellulose than an acre of poplar trees, the density of the material produced inefficiencies in the manufacturing process.[392] These inefficiencies could not be immediately overcome with the existing technology.

Ford eventually realized his dream of "growing" a car. In 1941, Ford demonstrated a prototype vehicle that included up to 10 percent hemp fiber encased in a plastic binder. But the car was not the "hemp car" advocates today promote. Additionally, the manufacturing processes used to construct it in 1941 were not scalable or feasible from a manufacturing cost perspective. This research was extremely valuable during World War II, however, as farm-based synthetic products like rubber made from alcohol substituted for materials no longer readily available.[393]

The unattributed promotional article "New Billion Dollar Crop," published in the February 1938 issue of *Popular Mechanics*, extolled the potential of hemp cellulose in manufacturing a variety of products. The article mentioned several businesses exploring opportunities in the hemp industry, including a "mill in Tilton, Illinois engaged in making paper."[394] The "mill" was a company named Amhempco, and within a year of the article's publication, Amhempco had sold its papermaking equipment.[395]

More important, Amhempco is a vital link to the Kentucky-Illinois Hemp Company.

AMHEMPCO

The Kentucky-Illinois Hemp Company's hempstory starts in Tilton, Illinois, the home of Amhempco. In 1934, the Ball Brothers, known for producing glass mason jars, acquired a fifty-acre industrial site in Illinois at an auction. The previous owner, a company named Cornstalks Products Company, had attempted to manufacture paper from the cellulose in cornstalks.[396]

The acquisition was enthusiastically reported in the local media. "It is the first time in the history of the plant, that it has been in the hands of men established in the manufacturing business. Never before has a company with the stability and financial backing of the Ball Brothers had control of the property."[397]

In February 1935, incorporation papers were filed in Delaware identifying the new venture as "Amhempco," a joint venture between the Balls Brothers and W.S. Sloane Company of New York. The filing stated the business planned to make "paper, etc." from hemp cellulose. This fit within the business models of the partner companies as the Ball Brothers already operated paper mills in several states, and W.S. Sloane used hemp fiber in the manufacture of linoleum and other products.[398]

The *Danville (IL) Commercial News* covered the Amhempco story. In the spring of 1935, it reported that organizers of the factory were seeking to contract for five thousand acres of hemp.[399] In August, the paper published a photograph of plant superintendent M.G. Moksnes in a test plot of hemp. Half of the field was planted with seed from Manchuria and the other half with seed from Kentucky. The article reported, "the best seed to use in this section is the Kentucky variety and not the Manchurian seed."[400] On October 13, the paper ran a feature on the first hemp harvest, conveying an overall sense of excitement about the potential prospects of a new industry.[401]

The year 1936 was a quiet one in terms of news for Amhempco, which only contracted local farmers to grow 1,200 acres of hemp. This hemp was used for research and development. The next year was extremely eventful and, as far as Amehempco was concerned, started on a high note. A headline in the *Danville Commercial News* declared that Tilton, Illinois, was poised to become the "Epicenter of American Hemp Industry."[402] The story, about the company open house, mentions several products, including plastics. More important in 1937, the paper reported that the factory would generate 110 new full-time and 75 seasonal jobs. Tilton was ready to be transformed by chemurgy.[403] However, before the *Commercial*

News ran these stories, two events in Washington, D.C., transpired to doom the future of Amhempco and any potential hemp industry renaissance.

In January 1936, the U.S. Supreme Court overturned the Agricultural Adjustment Act of 1932. This controversial New Deal program introduced price supports for various agricultural products whose markets suffered from oversupply.[404] The termination of the AAA resulted in a 40 percent drop[405] in the price of cotton the following year. Cotton competed with hemp as a source of fiber and cellulose. With cheap cotton available, many potential markets closed to hemp.

If the drop in cotton prices pushed Amhempco into a coffin, the Conference on Cannabis Sativa L., held at the U.S. Treasury Department in January 14, 1937, closed the coffin. The purpose of the conference was to discuss definitions of key terms to be used in the Marihuana Tax Act of 1937, which was ratified by Congress in late summer 1937. Attending the conference were several scientists employed or contracted by the federal government, director of the Federal Bureau of Narcotics Harry Anslinger, various officials within the Treasury Department and retired government agronomist Lyster H. Dewey. The purpose of the conference may have been to establish the language for the Marihuana Tax Act, but significant discussion ensued regarding the legitimate uses of hemp and markets in need of protection, including the hemp fiber, seed oil and bird seed industries. Conference attendees had more concerns about potential damage to the birdseed industry than to the fiber industry.[406]

That August, representatives of the hemp industry testified at Senate hearings on HR 6906, The Marihuana Tax of 1937. Five hemp processors attended, two from Wisconsin, two from Minnesota and Amhempco. There was no apparent coordination by these businesses to review the proposed legislation for potential threats to the industry and make a prepared joint statement. Only the two companies from Minnesota were represented by an attorney, and only the two companies from Wisconsin were established businesses. All of the companies seemed to have two concerns. First, business classification and the related financial exposure. And second, that the tax not be prohibitive to the small farmer.[407]

At this point there was a huge misunderstanding between the hemp industry and the authors of the proposed legislation. The five hemp mill owners were interested in processing hemp stalks into fiber and hurds. They didn't care about marihuana, the "flowering tops and leaves."[408] They considered the flowers and leaves waste. Their farmers cut the plant before it ripened and allowed the hemp to *rot* in the fields for two to six weeks. But legislators and

U.S. Treasury agents had interest in fully understanding the harvest and "retting" process. They knew that the hemp industry needed mature stalks and, during this meeting, were assured by industry representatives that the retting process destroyed any marihuana.

The reality was that leaving the plants to rot in the field did not physically destroy the plant's "flowering tops." Hemp cut and left in stacks in fields of Minnesota from the 1934–35 grow seasons still had degraded foliage attached when inspected by field agents in 1938. By strict definition, this was marihuana. And since the active compound in cannabis was unknown in 1937, all flowering tops, no matter how old and degraded, were considered marihuana. This created a problem for most processors when they purchased hemp from farmers. There was a "transfer tax."

By design, the tax act was intended to criminalize the sale of marihuana by taxing the transaction. The transfer tax was set at one dollar per ounce.[409] If the marihuana was not destroyed by the harvesting and retting process, then by law the sale of "hemp" from farmer to processor was a taxable exchange. The mathematics made the hemp industry financially unviable. In 1937, Amhempco contracted for five thousand acres of hemp at fifteen dollars per ton from local farmers.[410] The applied transfer tax was one dollar per ounce. The tax on one pound of hemp was more than the price on one ton. In 1937, local farmers produced a bumper crop, reported between ten thousand and fifteen thousand tons. The tax rate made sale of the crop financially unfeasible.

By the end of 1937, the nails were in Amhempco's coffin. In early December, one of the key buildings was damaged and several pieces of proprietary equipment destroyed in what the *Danville Commercial News* called a "suspicious" fire.[411] By the start of 1938, Amhempco existed solely to process its inventory of hemp and find a buyer for the fiber so the firm could attempt to pay its farmers. This goal was hampered by unresolved questions surrounding the transfer tax. Hemp industry executives appealed to the Federal Bureau of Narcotics (FBN), which did not believe changing the interpretation of the law was within its jurisdiction. The bureau's position was that hemp industry executives participated in the congressional hearings and their suggestions incorporated into the final legislation, approved by hemp industry executives. The duty of the bureau was to enforce the law as written.

Throughout 1939–40, Moksnes continued working to find legal ways to process and sell the hemp for which Amhempco had contracted. The company was in receivership and attempting to pay area farmers. In

December 1940, Moksnes and a representative of Kentucky River Mills met with FBN director Harry J. Anslinger to discuss the acquisition of Amhempco by Kentucky River Mills. Their discussion focused on creating a legal entity by which the remaining inventory of hemp in Danville, Illinois, could be handled without incurring the transfer tax. Director Anslinger was not insensitive to the situation, closing his letter, "I venture to express the hope that the desired result may be accomplished, to the satisfaction of all parties concerned."[412]

The February 15, 1941 *Danville Commercial News* reported that the Amhempco plant had closed and the equipment would be moved to a "new location somewhere near Frankfort KY, where it will be used to process hemp grown in that section," an area "recognized for its high-quality hemp."[413] Throughout spring 1941, Lexington, Paris and Versailles all lobbied to become the site of the relocated factory.

Kentucky-Illinois Hemp Company, Versailles, Kentucky, circa 1942. This breaking plant supplied hemp to Kentucky River Mills in Frankfort. *National Archives file 94533220.*

Matchbook promoting the businesses of D.D. Stewart, including Kentucky River Mills and the Kentucky-Illinois Hemp Company. *Courtesy Bill Reinke.*

Versailles, about fifteen miles from Frankfort, was selected as the site for the Kentucky-Illinois Hemp Company breaking plant. A subsidiary of Frankfort cordage manufacturer Kentucky River Mills, the Kentucky-Illinois Hemp Company supplied KRM with hemp fiber. Both facilities were featured in the last five minutes of the 1942 film *Hemp for Victory*. M.G. Moksnes initially served as the secretary and treasurer for Kentucky-Illinois Hemp before accepting a position as district supervisor with War Hemp Industries, the company coordinating the federal government's wartime hemp program.[414]

Three of the Versailles breaking plant buildings survive and are visible from the Versailles bypass on US 60. Hemp was decorticated in the Versailles facility and the fiber sent to Frankfort to be manufactured into twine. The Kentucky-Illinois Hemp Company closed following World War II.

AFTERWORD

Following the war, Congress corrected problems in the "transfer tax" section of the Marihuana Tax Act that crippled the hemp industry. It amended the law, exempting licensed growers and millers from the transfer tax.[415] However, even with these changes, the American hemp industry barely survived a decade following the end of the Second World War. Kentucky's last hemp mill, Kentucky River Mills ceased operation in 1952. The last hemp processor in the United States, Mat Rens and Company of Racine, Wisconsin, processed its last crop in 1958.[416]

Cannabis "hemp" was forgotten while public attention focused on cannabis "marihuana." Scientific understanding of cannabis in the 1950s was very limited. The psychoactive effects of some types of cannabis would only start to be unraveled in 1961, when Israeli scientist Dr. Raphael Mechoulam isolated the active compound in cannabis, delta-9-tetrahyrdocannabinal (THC).

By the mid-1960s and into the 1970s, hemp was seemingly forgotten as "marijuana" use became a banner for youth and the counterculture. Over time, Kentucky folklore grew rich with tales of outlaw growers and smugglers operating out of the hollows and hills across the state.

Hemp made a return to Kentucky's political consciousness in the 1990s, when Lexington attorney Gatewood Galbraith mounted several unsuccessful gubernatorial campaigns centered on a platform promoting "industrial hemp." Responding to the increased awareness and educational campaigns by industrial hemp advocates, in 1994, Kentucky governor Brereton Jones created a hemp task force to "consider the feasibility of this

In 1995, Lexington attorney Gatewood Galbraith's gubernatorial run attracted national support, including from country music legend and hemp advocate Willie Nelson.

historic crop." The panel superficially followed up on campaign promises Jones had made to study hemp. The panel, with a significant representation from law enforcement, "only met twice and voted 12-4 against further consideration."[417]

But, by 2014, enough momentum had gathered that federal guidelines for the first state hemp pilot programs were included in the 2014 Farm Bill.

The widespread acceptance and use of CBD as a legitimate therapeutic helped make most state pilot programs, including Kentucky's, successful. "Industrial hemp" was fully legalized in the 2018 Farm Bill. Once again, hemp farms dot the Kentucky landscape.

As part of the pilot program, new products are being developed across the commonwealth, utilizing Kentucky's longtime cash crop. Zelios in Lexington, Kentucky, uses a supercritical CO_2 process to extract CBD and other cannabinoids from hemp. The facility is Good Manufacturing Practices and kosher certified and offers a variety of products, from full spectrum oils to CBD isolate.

Victory Foods in Carrollton removes the shell from hemp seed, leaving a food that is nutritious and protein dense.

CBD, a therapeutic compound that occurs naturally in "industrial hemp," is extracted using a CO_2 process at Zelios Inc. *Courtesy Zelios Inc.*

Hemp stalks converted into eco-friendly Hempwood brand home flooring at the Hempwood pilot plant in Murray, Kentucky. *Courtesy Fibonacci LLC.*

Above: Hempwood also produces hempwood blocks for making table tops and decorative bowls. *Courtesy Fibonacci LLC*.

Left: A butterfly blesses the hemp industry renaissance in Kentucky.

Fibonacci's Hempwood pilot factory in Murray, Kentucky, converts hemp stalks into building materials such as hempwood flooring and hempwood blocks suitable for furniture fabrication.

At the start of the twenty-first century, we may be witnessing the dawn of a hemp renaissance in Kentucky.

NOTES

Introduction

1. Hopkins, *History of the Hemp Industry in Kentucky*, i.
2. "Hemp in Kentucky," Roadside Historical Marker, Kentucky Historical Society, accessed September 6, 2016, https://history.ky.gov/resources/publications-databases/historical-marker-database.

Chapter 1

3. Conrad, *Hemp Lifeline to the Future*, 6.
4. Dewey, "Hemp," 283.
5. Ibid., 283–84.
6. Ibid., 283.
7. Ibid., 287.
8. Ibid., 294–95.
9. Ibid., 287.
10. Hopkins, *History of the Hemp Industry in Kentucky*, 68.
11. Ibid., 69.
12. Ibid.
13. Ibid.
14. Ibid., 71.
15. Ibid., 50.

16. Ibid.
17. Dewey, "Hemp," 327.
18. Ibid.
19. Ibid., 328.
20. Ibid., 61.
21. Ibid.
22. Ibid.

Chapter 2

23. Dewey, "Hemp," 69.
24. "First Crop," Roadside Historical Marker, Kentucky Historical Society, accessed September 6, 2016, https://history.ky.gov/resources/publications-databases/historical-marker-database.
25. Clark, *History of Kentucky*, 26.
26. Ibid., 33.
27. Ibid., 37.
28. Collins, *History of Kentucky*, 452.
29. Collins and Collins, *Collins' Historical Sketches of Kentucky*, 519.
30. Ibid., 514.
31. Neal O. Hammon, "Early Kentucky Land Records, 1773–1780," Fincastle County, Virginia Genealogy and History, https://genealogy.com/va/fincastle/fincastlecommissionerland.html.
32. Collins, *History of Kentucky*, 204–05.
33. Larry E. Barnes, "Gen. Thomas Barbee," Find a Grave, accessed August 30, 2020, https://www.findagrave.com.
34. "Adams House, Danville, Kentucky," Kentucky Historical Society Colonial Dames Lantern Slides Graphic 19, accessed February 11, 2021, https://kyhistory.com/digital/collection/PH/id/730.
35. Fackler, *Early Days in Danville*, 51–53.
36. Barnes, "Gen. Thomas Barbee," Find A Grave.
37. Julie Kemper, "Dennis and Diadamia Doram: A View of the American Dream," Kentucky Ancestors, https://kentuckyancestors.org.
38. Blaine J. Hudson, "Afro-American Education," in Kleber, *Kentucky Encyclopedia*, 285.
39. Kemper, "Dennis and Diadamia Doram."
40. Ibid.
41. Ibid.
42. Ibid.

43. Brenda Edwards, "Man's Letters Told of Kentucky in 1800s," *Danville (KY) Advocate Messenger*, January 19, 1992.

44. Ibid.

45. Ibid.

46. Ibid.

47. Fackler, *Early Days in Danville*, 121.

48. Edwards, "Man's Letters Told of Kentucky."

49. Hopkins, *History of the Hemp Industry in Kentucky*, 120.

50. Edwards, "Man's Letters Told of Kentucky."

51. Ibid.

52. Sallie Bright, "Looking Back: Building Housed Bustling Hemp Cleaning Operation," *Danville Advocate Messenger*, May 9, 1993.

53. Ibid.

54. "Hudson and Davis," *Danville Advocate*, December 15, 1911.

55. "This Agreement Made This 23rd Day of September, 1916," historic document in Bluegrass Heritage Museum Hemp exhibit, Winchester, Kentucky.

56. Barbara Edwards, "Boyle Was a Leading County in Hemp Growing," *Danville Advocate Messenger*, June 14, 2019.

57. Ibid.

Chapter 3

58. "Bourbon County Hemp/Alexander House," Roadside Historical Marker, Kentucky Historical Society, accessed October 15, 2020, https://history.ky.gov/resources/publications-databases/historical-marker-database.

59. Collins, *History of Kentucky*, 192.

60. Hopkins, *History of the Hemp Industry in Kentucky*, 112.

61. Ibid.

62. "Bourbon County Hemp/Alexander House," Roadside Historical Marker, Kentucky Historical Society, accessed October 15, 2020, https://history.ky.gov/resources/publications-databases/historical-marker-database.

63. Hopkins, *History of the Hemp Industry in Kentucky*, 127.

64. Amanda Bradley Dee, "Cooper's Run Rural Historic District Bourbon County, Kentucky," National Register of Historic Places registration form, August 1, 1998.

65. Captain E.F. Spears and Sarah Woodford Spears obituaries, Kentucky Kindred Genealogical Research, September 11, 2016, https://kentuckykindredgenealogy.com.

66. Ibid.

67. Correspondence and Query Letters from Woodford Spears and Sons, Spears Family Papers, University of Kentucky Special Collections Library.

68. Letter to Woodford Spears and Sons, August 22, 1929, Spears Family Papers, University of Kentucky Special Collections Library.

69. Letter to Woodford Spears and Sons, April 19, 1939, Spears Family Papers, University of Kentucky Special Collections Library.

70. Telegram to Woodford Spears and Sons, September 9, 1939, Spears Family Papers University of Kentucky Special Collections Library.

71. Letter and Bill of Lading to Smith and Bird, November 9, 1939, Spears Family Papers University of Kentucky Special Collections Library.

72. Letter to Woodford Spears and Sons, December 6, 1939, Spears Family Papers University of Kentucky Special Collections Library.

73. Letter to Frank W. Bird Smith and Bird Co., December 9, 1939, Spears Family Papers University of Kentucky Special Collections.

74. The donation was completed just prior to the COVID-19 lockdown of 2020. As of this writing, the documents had not been sorted or catalogued. This volume is literally the first exploration of those records. Special access was granted to the author since he arranged the donation.

75. Margo Warminski, "Downtown Paris Historic District," National Register of Historic Places registration form, June 1989.

Chapter 4

76. "Clark County Hemp," Roadside Historical Marker, Kentucky Historical Society, accessed September 6, 2016, https://history.ky.gov/resources/publications-databases/historical-marker-database.

77. Harry Enoch, "Where in the World: Growing Hemp in Clark County," *Winchester (KY) Sun*, January 17, 2020.

78. Hopkins, *History of the Hemp Industry in Kentucky*, 64.

79. Goff A. Bedford, "Clark County," in Kleber, *Kentucky Encyclopedia*, 197.

80. Collins, *History of Kentucky*, 234.

81. Harry G. Enoch, "Where in the World: Hemp Manufacturing in Winchester," *Winchester (KY) Sun*, January 31, 2020.

82. Harry G. Enoch, "V.W. Bush Warehouse," in *Where in the World*, vol. 3, *Historic People and Places in Clark County, Kentucky* (Winchester, KY: Bluegrass Heritage Museum, 2018), 225.

83. Ibid., 219

84. Whitney Legget, "History of the V.W. Bush Warehouse," *Winchester (KY) Sun*, December 27, 2017.

85. Ibid.

86. Enoch, "V.W. Bush Warehouse," 226.

87. Harry G. Enoch, *A Tour of Places No Longer Here: The Parking Lots of Winchester* (Winchester, KY: Bluegrass Heritage Museum, 2016).

88. *Annual Reports of the Navy Department for the Year 1901: Report of the Secretary of the Navy* (Washington, D.C.: Government Printing Office, 1901), 1136.

89. *Annual Reports of the Navy Department for the Year 1903: Report of the Secretary of the Navy* (Washington, D.C.: Government Printing Office, 1903), 1158.

90. Enoch, "Where in the World: Growing Hemp in Clark County."

91. Ibid.

92. Ibid.

93. Hopkins, *History of the Hemp Industry in Kentucky*, 210–11.

94. Ibid., 211–12.

95. B.B. Robinson, "Hemp," *Farmers Bulletin* no. 1935 (Washington, D.C.: Government Printing Office, 1943).

96. Jack Herer, "Hemp for Victory," United States Department of Agriculture film, 1942, transcript reprinted in *The Emperor Wears No Clothes* (Van Nuys, CA: Hemp/Queen of Clubs Publishing, 1993), 123.

97. Hopkins, *History of the Hemp Industry in Kentucky*, 212.

98. David P. West, "Hemp in Wisconsin," Newhead News, https://www.newheadnews.com, updated version of an article that originally appeared in *Hemp World Magazine* (Winter 1998).

99. Hopkins, *History of the Hemp Industry in Kentucky*, 213.

100. Ibid., 213.

Chapter 5

101. Collins, *History of Kentucky*, 263–64.

102. Hopkins, *History of the Hemp Industry in Kentucky*, 113–14.

103. Charles T. Ambrose, "Transylvania University and Its Hemp Connection," *Microbiology, Immunology and Molecular Genetics Faculty Publications* 60 (2015): 12–13, https://uknowldegge.uky.edu/micorbio_facpub/60.

104. Clark, *History of Kentucky*, 31–32.

105. Joe Nickell, "Daniel Boone," in Kleber, *Encyclopedia of Kentucky*, 96.

106. "Capt. Morgan Bryan," Genealogy Corner, Find a Grave, accessed October 18, 2020, https://wwwfindagrave.com.

107. Nickell, "Daniel Boone," 97.

108. Ibid.

109. Anita J. Sanford, "Bryan's (Bryant's) Station," *Encyclopedia of Kentucky*, 133–34.

110. Collins, *History of Kentucky*, 268.

111. Hopkins, *History of the Hemp Industry in Kentucky*, 70.

112. Collins, *History of Kentucky*, 271.

113. "Butler's Rangers & Indian Department Captain Caldwell's Report," On-Line Institute for Advanced Loyalist Studies, https://royalprovincial.com.

114. Ibid.

115. Kathleen Arnold, "Daniel Boone Bryan Sr.," Find a Grave, accessed October 18, 2020, https://www.findagrave.com.

116. David Reese, "Joseph Bryan," Find a Grave, accessed October 18, 2020, https://www.findagrave.com.

117. Amy Murrell Taylor, "Slavery at Waveland: A Collaborative Effort of Students Enrolled in HIS 595" (final report), Slavery and Public History, University of Kentucky, April 2017, 7.

118. Sara L. Farley, "Waveland," in Kleber, *Kentucky Encyclopedia*, 938.

119. Hockensmith, "Eli Cleveland's Grist, Saw and Hemp Mills," 7.

120. Harper, *Unsettling the West*, 161.

121. Ibid.

122. Ibid., 161–62.

123. Ibid., 162.

124. Ibid.

125. Hockensmith, "Eli Cleveland's Grist, Saw and Hemp Mills," 8.

126. Ibid., 9–10.

127. "Fayette County Hemp," Roadside Historical Marker, Kentucky Historical Society, https://history.ky.gov/resources/publications-databases/historical-marker-database.

128. Ramage, *John Wesley Hunt*, 13–14.

129. Ibid., 21–23.

130. Ibid., 60.

131. Ibid.

132. Ibid., 37.

133. Ibid., 60–61.

134. Ibid., 69.

135. "Athens of the West," National Park Service, https://nps.gov.

136. Ramage, *John Wesley Hunt*, 68–69.

137. Ibid., 91.

138. Ibid., 94.

139. Ibid., 87.

140. "Hopemont," VisitLex, https://visitlex.com.

141. Melba Porter Hay, "Henry Clay," in Kleber, *Kentucky Encyclopedia*, 200.

142. Ibid.

143. Ibid.

144. Ibid.

145. Ibid., 201.

146. Hopkins, *History of the Hemp Industry in Kentucky*, 11–18.

147. "Letter to A.M. January and Sons," Hemp Collection, Kentucky Gateway Museum Center Library, https://www.kygmc.org.

148. "Historic Downtown Lexington Gratz Park Walking Tour," Heritage Hemp Trail, Kentucky Hemp Heritage Alliance Inc., 2017, https://www.heritagehemptrail.com.

149. "John Hunt Morgan (1825–1864)," Roadside Historical Marker, Kentucky Historical Society, accessed September 9, 2016, https://history.ky.gov/resources/publications-databases/historical-marker-database.

150. Ramage, *Rebel Raider*, 9.

151. Ibid., 10–11.

152. Ibid., 12.

153. Ibid., 18.

154. Ibid., 14.

155. John D. Wright Jr. and Eric H. Christianson, "Transylvania University," in Kleber, *Kentucky Encyclopedia*, 895.

156. Ramage, *Rebel Raider*, 19.

157. Ibid.

158. Ibid., 20.

159. Ibid., 23–24.

160. Ibid., 27–28.

161. Ibid., 30.

162. Ibid.

163. Ibid., 31.

164. Ibid., 32.

165. Ibid., 33.

166. Ibid., 36.

167. Ibid., 39.

168. Ibid., 41.

169. Ibid., 42–44.

170. Ibid., 40.
171. Ibid., 44–45.
172. Ibid., 50.
173. Ibid., 81–82.
174. Ibid., 82
175. Ibid., 87
176. Ibid., 111–12.
177. Ibid., 119.
178. Ibid., 215.
179. Ibid.
180. Ibid., 222–23.
181. Ibid., 237–38.
182. Ibid., 250.
183. Ibid., 250–51.
184. Ibid., 256–57.
185. Ambrose, "Transylvania University and Its Hemp Connection," 2.
186. Ibid.
187. Ibid., 3.
188. Ibid., 7.
189. Collins, *History of Kentucky*, 277.
190. Ambrose, "Transylvania University and Its Hemp Connection," 8.
191. Horace Holley, *A Discourse Occasioned by the Death of Colonel James Morrison* (Lexington, KY: J. Bradford, 1823).
192. Hopkins, *History of the Hemp Industry in Kentucky*, 75.
193. Ambrose, "Transylvania University and Its Hemp Connection," 8.
194. Ibid., 9.
195. "Benjamin Gratz," in Kleber, *Kentucky Encyclopedia*, 383.
196. Burton Milward and Mrs. George Foster, "Gratz Park Historic District," National Register of Historic Places, inventory nomination form, March 14, 1973.
197. "Benjamin Gratz," Civil War Governors of Kentucky Digital Documentary Edition, accessed February 23, 2021, http://discovery.civilwargovernors.org.
198. Ibid.
199. Hopkins, *History of the Hemp Industry in Kentucky*, 135.
200. "Benjamin Gratz," in Kleber, *Kentucky Encyclopedia*, 381.
201. Jeremy D. Popkin, "My Benjamin Gratz Problem—and Ours," transcript of presentation, September 24, 2020, University of Kentucky, Department of History, October 9, 2020, Zoom presentation in conjunction with the Jewish Studies Program.

202. Hopkins, *History of the Hemp Industry in Kentucky*, 119–20.

203. Ibid., 120.

204. Ibid., 123.

205. Zanne Jefferies, "312 North Limestone St.," in *Constitution* (Lexington, KY: Blue Grass Trust for Historic Preservation, 2008), 26–27.

206. Milton Thompson Sr., "Rose Hill: The John Brand House," National Register of Historic Places, inventory nomination form, December 30, 1974.

207. Hopkins, *History of the Hemp Industry in Kentucky*, 117.

208. Thompson, "Rose Hill."

209. Hopkins, *History of the Hemp Industry in Kentucky*, 127.

210. Ibid.

211. Thompson, "Rose Hill."

212. Ibid.

213. "Historic Downtown Lexington Gratz Park Walking Tour," Heritage Hemp Trail, 2017.

214. Ibid.

215. Ramage, *Rebel Raider*, 30.

216. "Brucetown—W.W. Bruce," North End Residents, North Limestone Community Development Company, accessed June 17, 2017, http://northlimestoneculturalplan.org.

217. "William Wallace Bruce," obituaries, *Chicago Tribune*, November 16, 1896.

218. James C. Klotter, "James Lane Allen," in Kleber, *Kentucky Encyclopedia*, 14.

219. Allen, *Kentucky Cardinal and Aftermath*, xxix–xxx.

220. Ibid.

Chapter 6

221. Collins, *History of Kentucky*, 303–5.

222. "Leestown," Roadside Historical Marker, Kentucky Historical Society, accessed June 4, 2019, https://history.ky.gov/resources/publications-databases/historical-marker-database.

223. Carl E. Kramer, "Leestown," in Kleber, *Kentucky Encyclopedia*, 542.

224. Johnson, *History of Franklin County*, 30.

225. Ibid., 9.

226. Ibid., 41.

227. Ibid., 53.

228. "Franklin County Hemp," Roadside Historical Marker, Kentucky Historical Society, accessed September 9, 2016, https://history.ky.gov/resources/publications-databases/historical-marker-database.

229. Coffey, *Paul Sawyier*, 16.

230. Johnson, *History of Franklin County*, 18.

231. "The Role of Twine in American Agriculture," Archive.org, www.bridoncordage.com\history_twine.html.

232. Johnson, *History of Franklin County*, 18.

233. "Role of Twine in American Agriculture."

234. Coffey, *Paul Sawyier*, 15.

235. Ibid., 16.

236. Ibid., 40.

237. Ibid., 155.

238. "D.D. Stewart Buys Hemp Mill," *Lexington (KY) Herald*, November 20, 1938.

239. Hopkins, *History of the Hemp Industry in Kentucky*, 6.

240. "Hemp Order of $148,000 Made by Navy," *Courier-Journal* (Louisville, KY), February 22, 1941.

241. Naval History and Heritage Command. "Wasp VIII (CV-7) 1940–1942." https://www.history.navy.mil/research/histories/ship-histories/dansf/w/wasp-vii.html.

Chapter 7

242. George H. Yater, "The Falls of the Ohio," in Kleber, *Kentucky Encyclopedia*, 305.

243. Collins, *History of Kentucky*, 354–56.

244. Ella Hutchinson Ellwanger, "Oxmoor—Its Builder and Its Historian," *Register of the Kentucky State Historical Society* 17, no. 49 (January 1919): 7–21, accessed February 5, 2021, https://www.jstor.org.

245. "William Christian," in Kleber, *Kentucky Encyclopedia*, 184–85.

246. Collins, *History of Kentucky*, 233.

247. "William Christian," 184–85.

248. Ibid.

249. Whitsitt, *Life and Times of Judge Caleb Wallace*, 73–79.

250. Collins, *History of Kentucky*, 231.

251. "Bullitt, Alexander Scott," in Kleber, *Kentucky Encyclopedia*, 139.

252. Hopkins, *History of the Kentucky Hemp Industry*, 69.

253. Ibid., 136.

254. "Farmington," Roadside Historical Marker, Kentucky Historical Society, accessed September 9, 2016, https://history.ky.gov/resources/publications-databases/historical-marker-database.

255. "Lt. James Speed," *Geni*, Daughters of the American Revolution, accessed September 6, 2020, https://www.geni.com.

256. "Speed, Joshua Fry," in Kleber, *Kentucky Encyclopedia*, 841.

257. Lakshmi Gandhi, "What Does 'Sold Down the River' Really Mean? The Answer Isn't Pretty," *Code Switch*, January 27, 2014, http://npr.org.

258. "The Election of 1860," U.S. History, accessed March 5, 2021, https://www.ushistory.org.

259. "The South Secedes," U.S. History, accessed March 5, 2021, https://www.ushistory.org.

260. "Speed, Joshua Fry," 841.

Chapter 8

261. "Jessamine County Hemp," Roadside Historical Marker, Kentucky Historical Society, accessed September 9, 2016, https://history.ky.gov/resources/publications-databases/historical-marker-database.

262. Ron D. Bryant, "Jessamine County," in Kleber, *Kentucky Encyclopedia*, 469.

263. Collins, *History of Kentucky*, 375–76.

264. Young, *History of Jessamine County, Kentucky*, 161.

265. Mary Cronan Oppel, "George I. Brown House (Edgewood)," National Register of Historic Places, inventory nomination form, May, 23, 1977.

266. Young, *History of Jessamine County, Kentucky*, 161.

267. Oppel, "George I. Brown House (Edgewood)."

268. Young, *History of Jessamine County, Kentucky*, 271.

269. "George Brown and Anne Hemphill Buried in Maple Grove Cemetery," Kentucky Kindred Genealogy, https://kentuckykindredgenealogy.com.

270. Young, *History of Jessamine County, Kentucky*, 271–72.

271. "Oliver Anderson Biography," Missouri State Parks, http://mostateparks.com.

272. Ibid.

273. Ibid.

274. Ibid.

275. Ibid.

276. Ibid.

277. Wood, *Siege of Lexington, Missouri*, 38–40.

278. "At Battle of Lexington State Historic Site," Missouri State Parks, http://mostateparks.com.

279. Ibid.

280. "The First Battle of Lexington," Wikia.org, https://military.wikia.org.

281. Ibid.

282. Ibid.

283. "Oliver Anderson Biography," Missouri State Parks.

284. Young, *History of Jessamine County*, 159–60.

285. Charlene Lichtman, "Payne-Saunders House," National Register of Historic Places registration form, June 19, 1996.

286. Young, *History of Jessamine County*, 254.

287. Lichtman, "Payne-Saunders House."

288. Ibid.

289. Young, *History of Jessamine County*, 255.

290. Sanborn Fire Insurance Map from Nicholasville, Jessamine County, Kentucky Sanborn Map Company October 1892, Library of Congress, www.loc.gov.

291. Ibid., October 1897.

292. Ibid., October 1903.

293. Sanborn Fire Insurance Map from Lexington, Fayette County, Kentucky Sanborn Map Company, December 1890, Library of Congress..

Chapter 9

294. Collins, *History of Kentucky*, 416–19.

295. "Madison Hemp and Flax Co.," Roadside Historical Marker, Kentucky Historical Society, accessed September 9, 2016, https://history.ky.gov/resources/publications-databases/historical-marker-database.

296. Hopkins, *History of the Hemp Industry in Kentucky*, 117–18.

297. Ibid., 74–75.

298. Hockensmith, "Tates Creek Mills," 11.

299. Ibid., 12.

300. Ibid.

301. Ibid.

302. Clark, *History of Kentucky*, 185.

Chapter 10

303. "Shelby County Hemp," Roadside Historical Marker, Kentucky Historical Society, accessed September 9, 2016, https://history.ky.gov/resources/publications-databases/historical-marker-database.

304. *Lexington (KY) Herald Leader*, May 21, 1989.

305. Ron D. Bryant, "Lewis Collins," in Kleber, *Kentucky Encyclopedia*, 214.

306. Ibid.

307. Collins, *History of Kentucky*, 428–33.

308. Ibid., 432–33.

309. A. Gwynn Henderson and Nancy O'Malley, "Ribbon of History: The Maysville to Lexington Road," *Heritage Spotlight*, no. 1 (2013), Kentucky Heritage Council, https://transportation.ky.gov.

310. Ibid.

311. "The 1824 Election and the Corrupt Bargain," U.S. History, accessed March 4, 2021, http://www.ushistory.org.

312. Clark, *A History of Kentucky*, 153.

313. Henderson, and O'Malley, "Ribbon of History."

314. "Letter to A.M. January and Sons," Hemp Collection.

315. "Adam Beatty (May 10, 1777–June 9, 1858), American Lawyer, Writer," World Biographical Encyclopedia, version 2.0.45.1040, 2020, https://prabook.com/web/adam.beatty/3765220.

316. *Report of the Kentucky State Agricultural Society to the Legislature of Kentucky for the Years 1856–57*, Kentucky State Agricultural Society, Frankfort, Kentucky, 7–8.

317. Hopkins, *History of the Hemp Industry in Kentucky*, 105.

318. Ibid., 16.

319. Phil Breen, "Pogue House," National Register of Historic Places registration form, October 6, 2005.

Chapter 11

320. "Hemp in Scott County," Roadside Historical Marker, Kentucky Historical Society, accessed September 9, 2016, https://history.ky.gov/resources/publications-databases/historical-marker-database.

321. Collins, *History of Kentucky*, 504.

322. "Georgetown," in Kleber, *Kentucky Encyclopedia*, 371.

323. Ira Birdwhistell, "Elijah Craig," in Kleber, *Kentucky Encyclopedia*, 238–39.

324. Leland R. Johnson, *Engineering the Kentucky River: The Commonwealth's Waterway* (Louisville, KY: U.S. Army Corps of Engineers, Louisville District, 1999), 9.

325. B.O. Gaines, *History of Scott County* (Georgetown, KY: B.O. Gaines Printery, 1905), 224.

326. Hopkins, *History of the Hemp Industry in Kentucky*, 114–15.

327. Georgetown and Scott County Museum, "The First Paper Mill in the United States 'Western Country': Craig, Parker and Company Big Spring Branch Georgetown, KY," Flyer compiled and distributed by Georgetown Scott County Museum.

328. Ibid.

329. Ibid.

330. Hopkins, *History of the Hemp Industry in Kentucky*, 113.

331. Ambrose, "Transylvania University and Its Hemp Connection," 19.

332. Gaines, *History of Scott County*, 249–50.

333. Ibid.

334. Ibid., 243.

335. Ann B. Bevins, "Tarleton House," Kentucky Historic Resources Inventory, Historic American Buildings Survey Inventory, 1970.

336. Owen Lourie, "Jeremiah Tarleton," Archives of Maryland: Biographical Series, 2018, http://msa.maryland.gov.

337. John Tarleton, "Jeremiah Tarleton," Family Genealogies, USGenWebsites, retrieved October 20, 2020, http://usgenwebsites.org.

338. Ann Bevins, "President's House: Harvey C. Graves," Kentucky Historic Resource Inventory, Historic American Buildings Survey Inventory, November 19, 1969.

339. Ann Bevins, "Annual Tour of Homes Mixes Holiday Cheer with History Lessons," *News Graphic* (Georgetown, KY), November 26, 2014, https://www.news-graphic.com.

340. Ibid.

341. Ibid.

342. Sanborn Fire Insurance Map from Georgetown, Scott County, Kentucky, Sanborn Map Company, May 1886, Library of Congress, https://www.loc.gov.

343. Ibid., December, 1890.

344. Ibid., October, 1895.

345. Ibid., October, 1907.

346. "Mr. Ezra N. Offutt Dies at Georgetown," *Lexington (KY) Herald*, June 27, 1911.

347. Hopkins, *History of the Hemp Industry in Kentucky*, 205–6.

348. Ibid., 206

349. Dewing, *History of the National Cordage Company*, 5.

350. Ibid., 5.

351. Ibid., 6.

352. Ibid., 7.

353. Ibid., 10.

354. Ibid., 9.

355. Ibid., 16.

356. Ibid., 18.

357. Ibid.

358. Ibid., 11.

359. Ibid., 10.

360. Ibid., 17.

361. Ibid., 20.

362. Ibid., 25.

363. Ibid., 22.

364. Ibid., 19.

365. Ibid.

366. Ibid., 32.

367. Ibid., 12.

368. Ibid., 10.

369. Ibid., 26.

370. Ibid., 29–30.

371. Ibid., 42.

372. Ibid., 1.

373. Bulletin 47, Replies to Tariff Inquiries, Schedule J., Flax, Hemp, Jute, and Manufacturers of Numbers 5595–5682, United States Senate, 53rd Congress, 2nd Session (Washington, D.C.: Government Printing Office, 1894), 3–4.

374. Ibid., 35–36.

375. Ibid.

376. *Georgetown (KY) Times*, May 4, 1904.

Chapter 12

377. Collins, *History of Kentucky*, 517–18.

378. "Shelby County Hemp," Roadside Historical Marker, Kentucky Historical Society, accessed September 9, 2016, https://history.ky.gov/resources/publications-databases/historical-marker-database.

379. "Hemp Ridge Road," *Louisville Courier-Journal*, March 2, 1950. https://heritagehemptrail.com/shelbycountyhemp?pgid=k9n97rf4-013ff957-7513-4df-af11-7038a10ad118.

380. Phillip Rice, "Kentucky Descendants of Rowlett Rice: Revolutionary War Soldier from Virginia," *Your Rice Family E-Zine* 3, no. 2, February 10, 2010, accessed February 12, 2021. https://archive.constantcontact.com/fs051/1101861701430/archive/11029935217577.html. The preceding website was reached by a Google keyword search of 'Kentucky Descendants for Rowlett Rice.' Search results lead to an "unsecured website." Author cautions enter at own risk.

381. Ibid.

382. C. Worsham, "William Sleadd Farm," Kentucky Historic Resources, individual inventory form, April 1986.

383. William H. Perrin, J.W. Battle and G.C. Kiffin, *Kentucky: A History of the State: Embracing a Concise Account of the Origin and Development of the Virginia Colony; Its Expansion Westward, and the Settlement of the Frontier* (Louisville, KY: Southern Historical Press, F.A. Battey and Company, 1887), 748. http://books,google.com.

384. Alyssa Erickson, "The History of Hemp in Shelby County," Shelby County Hemp exhibit, accessed February 12, 2021, https://shelbykyhistory.org.

385. Perrin, Battle and Kiffin, *Kentucky: A History of the State*, 753.

386. Hopkins, *History of the Hemp Industry in Kentucky*, 126.

387. Ibid., 127.

388. Ibid.

Chapter 13

389. Collins, *History of Kentucky*, 552–54.

390. "Woodford County Hemp," Roadside Historical Marker, Kentucky Historical Society, accessed September 6, 2016, https://history.ky.gov/resources/publications-databases/historical-marker-database.

391. Finlay, "Old Efforts at New Uses," 33–46.

392. Lyster H. Dewey and Jason L. Merrill, "USDA Bulletin 404: Hemp Hurds as Papermaking Material" (Washington, D.C.: U.S. Government Printing Office, 1916), 22–23.

393. Finaly, "Old Efforts at New Uses," 39.

394. "New Billion Dollar Crop," *Popular Mechanics*, February 1938, 238–39, 144A–145A.

395. "Amhempco Sells Mill Machinery," *Commercial News* (Danville, IL), December 10, 1939.

396. "Chicago Broker Highest Bidder," *Commercial News*, August 30, 1934.

397. "Tilton Property Sold to Company of Muncie, IND," *Commercial News*, September 5, 1934.

398. State of Delaware Annual Report, Delaware Corporation, January 4, 1938.

399. "Complete Sign Up of Hemp Acreage to Produce Crop for Use at Tilton Plant: Total of 5,000 Acres Expected to Produce 15,000 Tons Next Fall," *Commercial News*, May 5, 1935.

400. "Public Can See Test of Hemp Crop near Here," *Commercial News*, August 8, 1935.

401. Hud Robbins, "Harvest of First Local Hemp Crop Is Nearing Close," *Commercial News*, October 13, 1935.

402. Hud Robbins, "New Epicenter of American Hemp Production," *Commercial News*, February 28, 1937.

403. Hud Robbins, "Offer New Products: Employ 110 Men," *Commercial News*, February 27, 1937.

404. "Agricultural Adjustment Act (1933, Reauthorized 1938)," The Living New Deal, https://www.livingnewdeal.org.

405. "Deny Hemp Plant to Close," *Commercial News*, October 1, 1937.

406. "Conference on Cannabis Sativa L. January 14, 1937," Drug Library, http://www.druglibrary.org.

407. "Taxation on Marihuana," hearing before a Senate Subcommittee of the Committee on Finance United States Senate, 75th Congress, 1st Session, H.R. 6906 (Washington, D.C.: U.S. Government Printing Office, 1937).

408. Ibid.

409. Ibid.

410. "Deny Hemp Plant to Close."

411. Hud Robbins, "Smoke of Amhempco Plant Fire Casts Pall over Prospects of Paying Growers for Huge Crop," *Commercial News*, December 12, 1937.

412. Correspondence, Harry J. Anslinger to R.D. Acton and M.G. Moksnes, December 1941, FOIA, Danville Public Library, Danville, Illinois.

413. "Amhempco Plant Will Move," *Commercial News*, February 15, 1938.

414. Bulletin #37, War Hemp Industries Inc., Chicago, Illinois, July 28, 1943.

Afterword

415. "Coverage of Certain Drugs Under the Federal Narcotics Laws," Congressional Record-House, February 28, 1946 (Washington, D.C.: Government Printing Office, 1946), 1760–62.
416. Dennis Rens, "America's Hemp King," Cornucopia Institute, 19, https://www.cornucopia.org.
417. Hopkins, *History of the Hemp Industry in Kentucky*, x.

BIBLIOGRAPHY

NOTE: Lewis Collins first published his seminal work, *Historical Sketches of Kentucky, History of Kentucky*, in 1847. In 1877, his son Richard revised and updated the volume in anticipation that it would be adopted by the commonwealth as an official history textbook. When it was rejected, Richard Collins published several editions on his own. The author has pulled from three distinct versions: a reprint of the original 1847 text published in 1968, a copy of an 1877 Richard Collins edition found online at Google Books, and an original copy of volume 1 from an 1878 Richard Collins edition.

The online Find a Grave database was utilized extensively to fill in biographical information and confirm lineage.

Allen, James Lane. *A Kentucky Cardinal and Aftermath.* New York: MacMillan Company, 1900.

Clark, Thomas D. *A History of Kentucky.* Ashland, KY: Jesse Stuart Foundation, 1988.

Coffey, William Donald. *Paul Sawyier: Kentucky Artist; An Historical Chronology of His Art, Friends and Times from Old Frankfort to the Catskills.* Frankfort, KY: Frankfort Heritage Press, 2010.

Collins, Lewis. *History of Kentucky.* Lexington, KY: Henry Clay Press, 1968.

Collins, Lewis, and Richard Collins. *Collins' Historical Sketches of Kentucky, History of Kentucky.* Vol. 1. Covington, KY: Collins & Company, 1878.

Conrad, Chris. *Hemp: Lifeline to the Future; The Unexpected Answer for Our Environmental and Economic Recovery.* Los Angeles: Creative Expressions Publications, 1994.

Crosby, Alfred W., Jr. *America, Russia, Hemp and Napoleon: American Trade with Russia and the Baltic, 1783–1812*. Columbus: Ohio State University Press, 1965.

Day, Grant L. "Kentucky River Mills Company's Hemp Mill." *Millstone: Journal of the Kentucky Old Mill Association* 2, no. 2 (Fall 2003): 15–26.

Dewey, Lyster H. "Hemp." *Yearbook of the United States Department of Agriculture, 1913*. Washington D.C.: Government Printing Office, 1914, 283–346.

Dewing, Arthur S. *A History of the National Cordage Company; With a Supplement Containing Copies of Important Documents*. Cambridge, MA: Harvard University Press, 1913.

Fackler, Calvin M. *Early Days in Danville*. Louisville, KY: Standard Print Company, 1941.

Finlay, Mark. "Old Efforts at New Uses: A Brief History of Chemurgy and the American Search for Biobased Materials." *Journal of Industrial Ecology* 7, no. 3–4 (2004): 33–46.

Harper, Rob. *Unsettling the West: Violence and State Building in the Ohio Valley*. Philadelphia: University of Pennsylvania Press, 2018.

Hockensmith, Charles. "Eli Cleveland's Grist, Saw and Hemp Mills (1793–1796) on Boone's Creek in Fayette County, Kentucky." *Millstone: Journal of the Kentucky Old Mill Association* 14, no. 2 (Fall 2015): 7–10.

Hockensmith, Charles. "The Tates Creek Mills: An Early Milling Complex in Madison County, Kentucky." *Millstone: Journal of the Kentucky Old Mill Association* 14, no. 2 (Fall 2015): 11–16.

Hopkins, James F. *A History of the Hemp Industry in Kentucky*. Lexington: University Press of Kentucky, 1998.

Johnson, Lewis Franklin. *History of Franklin County, KY*. Frankfort, KY: Roberts Printing Company, 1912.

Kleber, John E., ed. *The Kentucky Encyclopedia*. Lexington: University Press of Kentucky, 1992.

Penn, William A. *The Civil War in Midway, Kentucky*. Midway, KY: Historic Midway Museum Store, 2012.

Ramage, James A. *John Wesley Hunt: Pioneer Merchant, Manufacturer and Financier*. Lexington: University Press of Kentucky, 1974.

———. *Rebel Raider: The Life of General John Hunt Morgan*. Lexington: University Press of Kentucky, 1986.

Wallis, Frederick A., and Tapp, Hambleton. *A Sesquicentennial History of Kentucky*. Hopkinsville, KY: Historical Record Association, 1945.

Whitsitt, William H. *Life and Times of Judge Caleb Wallace*. Louisville, KY: John P. Morton & Company, 1888.

Wood, Larry. *The Siege of Lexington, Missouri: The Battle of the Hemp Bales*. Charleston, SC: The History Press. 2014.

Young, Bennet H. *A History of Jessamine County, Kentucky from Its Earliest Settlement to 1898*. Louisville, KY: Courier Journal Job Printing, 1898.

INDEX

ABOUT THE AUTHOR

An unabashed history nerd, Dan Isenstein started doing serious research into cannabis hemp while a graduate student in the Popular Culture Studies program at Bowling Green State University. *Tales from the Hemp Highway of Kentucky*, Dan's first book, builds on his research used in creating the self-directed eponymous tour launched in 2016. In addition to research and writing, Dan also chaired the organizing committee for the inaugural Winchester Hemp Harvest Festival in 2019 and has authored several articles about hemp in *Terpenes and Testing Magazine*. Dan also hosts "Hemp Threads: Weaving an Industry" on the Hemp Highway of Kentucky YouTube channel.

LinkedIn: linkedin.com/in/hemp-highway-of-kentucky
Twitter: @HempHighwayKY
Facebook: Hemp Highway of Kentucky
Medium: @dan-68157
YouTube: Hemp Highway of Kentucky
IG: hemphighwayky